Praise for *Evolving with Gratitude*

The science and practice of gratitude have evolved by leaps and bounds in recent years. You and your family can also evolve with gratitude, and Lainie Rowell shows how. Informational and inspirational, the book blends the best research and practices with Lainie's own personal experiences. Lainie's transparency lends an air of honesty and humility to the wisdom she dispenses and will assist you in living joyfully, effectively, and meaningfully. She clearly and compellingly demonstrates that gratitude is the best approach to life!

—**Robert Emmons**, editor-in-chief of *The Journal of Positive Psychology* and author of *Thanks!: How the New Science of Gratitude Can Make You Happier*

Inspiring. Practical. Actionable. The perfect book to help you bring more gratitude into your own life and your learning communities.

—**Marc Brackett**, PhD, bestselling author of *Permission to Feel* and founding director of the Yale Center for Emotional Intelligence

Evolving with Gratitude highlights the vital role of a positive mindset in facing life's challenges, and Rowell provides insightful and practical ways of moving gratitude from a moment to a habit.

—**Shawn Achor**, *New York Times* bestselling author of *Big Potential* and *The Happiness Advantage*

Evolving with Gratitude is the guide every teacher and leader needs to find their true purpose in this work. If we are not intentional and purposeful about the impact we make in our daily lives, it will be very difficult to serve and empower others. In this amazing book, the author teaches us the keys to improving our relationships with students and appreciating our blessings every day.

—**Salome Thomas-EL**, award-winning principal and author

Brilliantly written and complete with activities, supporting research, and stories from the field, this book will equip you to make a significant impact. Practicing gratitude can positively transform learning environments in ways that can cause a ripple effect.

—**Elisabeth Bostwick**, award-winning educator and author of *Take the L.E.A.P.: Ignite a Culture of Innovation*

In *Evolving with Gratitude*, Lainie Rowell doesn't only discuss the feel-good emotions linked to gratitude, she also brings in the neuroscience of how our brains change with a regular gratitude practice to back up her claims. Incorporate her pragmatic, simple gratitude strategies and practices, and you'll find yourself feeling seriously thankful that you read her book.

—**Mandy Froehlich**, education consultant, Divergent EDU

Lainie Rowell does a masterful job of weaving together story and practice. I found myself reflecting on how I got to this place and, more importantly, how I could walk with more purpose. I highly recommend it not only to educators but to anyone who wants to provide value to those around them.

—**Joe Sanfelippo**, superintendent, author, and speaker

What a refreshing return to the simple things in life, love, and especially work that will have ripple effects on well-being in our schools and society. Lainie Rowell has been a trailblazer in our space over the last two decades and shows us that innovation—the practical application of ideas to improve or create new goods and services—isn't very complicated. Equifinality!

—**David Miyashiro**, EdD, superintendent, Cajon Valley Union School District

WOW. This book has expanded my capacity for creative thinking and positive culture. Lainie Rowell and the contributors have given me practical strategies for growing my gratitude and that of others. Gratitude is much more than saying thank you and being polite. This is a must-read to uncover the true magic behind gratitude and how it can unlock our greatest potential.

—**Meghan Lawson**, educational leader and writer

Evolving with Gratitude reads like a warm blanket on a snowy day. Lainie Rowell combines inspiration and stories, allowing educators to reflect on their life's journey. With the chaos of life these days, this book provides the proper perspective to keep our eyes up and hearts filled for our true life's calling.

—**Neil Gupta**, district administrator

What a beautiful book! I connected to the stories that Lainie and the contributors shared, I delighted in checking out the valuable resources included in the book, and I cannot wait to try out many of the ideas suggested. To wake up every morning grateful for the opportunities that lie ahead is a blessing, and Lainie does a brilliant job describing the benefits of gratitude in an incredibly heartwarming and engaging fashion.

—**Allyson Apsey**, educational leader, author, speaker

Evolving with Gratitude is the social-emotional GPS for twenty-first-century leaders who serve. Lainie Rowell seamlessly navigates the realistic terrain of emotion, fatigue, and legacy with a clear lens that shows us exactly how to embrace the scenery of the journey while circumventing the potholes, detours, and road closures. From developing powerful daily habits to public displays of gratitude, *Evolving with Gratitude* is a must-read!

—**Dr. Mary Hemphill**, founder and CEO of The Limitless Leader and Eduprenuer

As someone who practices gratitude, I came upon this book thinking it would merely reinforce some of my own practices. I had no idea how much more I had to learn! In *Evolving with Gratitude,* Lainie Rowell combines research and strategies, using her own rich experiences. The book is full of insights and ideas from respected thought leaders across the globe. This is a must-read for any educator in any role who cares deeply about our kids and wants to help them connect to the world more positively and gratefully.

—**Jennifer Casa-Todd**, educator, author, and keynote speaker

Through quotes, research, practical ideas, and stories from educators, Lainie Rowell shares strategies for practicing gratitude that strengthen the neural pathways and increase happiness. I highly recommend *Evolving with Gratitude* for educators who want to foster a culture of gratitude that empowers kids to be agents of change who make the world a better place.

—**Barbara Bray**, creative learning strategist, podcast host, and author of *Define Your Why*

As educational leaders, we are charged with having answers or knowing where to find them. The past two years have been among the most difficult of my twenty-nine years as an educator but have also made me realize the importance of human interaction and gratitude. *Evolving with Gratitude* is a reminder that, above all, people and relationships come first.

—**Jerry Almendarez**, superintendent, Santa Ana USD

Educators who want to show up in the most positive and productive of ways will benefit from reading *Evolving with Gratitude*. Practical, applicable, accessible—you will love it!

—**Amber Teamann**, director of technology and innovation, Crandall ISD

Once again, Lainie Rowell proves why she is an up-and-coming star in educational literature. *Evolving with Gratitude* is a practical, easy-to-read resource for educators who are looking for actionable habits to implement in daily life. Do yourself a favor and add it to your book list!

—**Dr. Jared Smith**, school superintendent and award-winning author

We are all given a choice in this life to be ungrateful critics or to be intentional in discovering, practicing, and sharing gratitude. Lainie Rowell sets forth not only the case for building gratitude habits but also multiple ways to embed the practice into our everyday lives. One of the greatest gifts of *Evolving with Gratitude* is modeling the practice with our students. As Lainie shares, "we can empower our kids to be agents of change who make the world a better place." *Evolving with Gratitude* is a great place to start!

—**Dr. Jill M. Siler**, TASA deputy executive director and author of *Thrive Through the Five*

Lainie delivers an inspiring and practical book to bring gratitude into our learning communities with practices that can be implemented immediately. Stories shared by educators in a variety of roles illustrate the power of cultivating a culture of authentic gratitude with kids, peers, and the world! You will want to keep this book handy so you can refer to it often for innovative ideas to establish learning environments where all thrive personally and academically.

—**Thomas C. Murray**, director of innovation, Future Ready Schools

Evolving with Gratitude

LAINIE ROWELL

EVOLVING
WITH
GRATITUDE

Small Practices in Learning Communities That Make
a Big Difference with Kids, Peers, and the World

Evolving with Gratitude: Small Practices in Learning Communities That Make a Big Difference with Kids, Peers, and the World
© 2022 Lainie Rowell

This book is available at special discounts when purchased in quantity for educational purposes or for use as premiums, promotions, or fundraisers. For inquiries and details, contact the publisher at books@impressbooks.org.

Published by IMPress, a division of Dave Burgess Consulting, Inc.
IMPressbooks.org
DaveBurgessConsulting.com
San Diego, CA

Library of Congress Control Number: 2022939435
Hardcover ISBN: 978-1-948334-59-4
Paperback ISBN: 978-1-948334-54-9
Ebook ISBN: 978-1-948334-55-6

Cover design by Allyson Liu Creative
Interior design by Liz Schreiter
Edited and produced by Reading List Editorial
ReadingListEditorial.com

For my husband, Lawrence, and our blessings, Kendall and Blake, I am profoundly grateful.

For those nurturing grateful hearts and minds.

Contents

Introduction   Why Gratitude?   1

Chapter 1   What Is Gratitude?   6

What Are the Benefits?   10

Equifinality   12

Chapter 2   Gratitude Practices   18

Gratitude in the Midst of Adversity   18

Gratitude for the Good in Life (and in Education)   23

Getting Started   27

Options for Everyone   28

Notice-Think-Feel-Do   38

Building Gratitude Habits   40

Chapter 3   Gratitude with Kids   45

First, Gratitude for Kids   45

Teaching Kids to Be Grateful   53

Grateful to Learn   54

A Thankful Learning Community   57

Gratitude at Every Age and Stage   58

Even More Gratitude Practices with Kids   71

Chapter 4 Gratitude with Peers   73

Profound Gratitude   73
Do We Have to Be Grateful for Everyone?   74
From Surviving to Thriving and Flourishing   76
Parents and Families as Peers   87
Honoring How Peers Are Unique and Dynamic   91
Reflecting on Gratitude with Peers   94

Chapter 5 Gratitude with the World   96

Kindness and Gratitude   96
Public Displays of Gratitude   99
Our Legacy for the Greater Good   109
Empowering Learners with Purpose   111

Conclusion Give a Shout-out   114

Resources We Can Be Grateful For   116
Notes   118
With Thanks   122
About the Author   126
About the Contributors   128
More from IMPRESS   135

INTRODUCTION

Why Gratitude?

> *I would maintain that thanks are the highest form of thought, and that gratitude is happiness doubled by wonder.*
>
> —G. K. Chesterton

"Ahem, what do you say?"

How many times do kids hear this growing up? It's a common prompt from adults for kids to say thank you (even when they don't necessarily appreciate something). The *hope* is that showing gratitude becomes ingrained in our littles, and they grow up to be good people with good manners. But how do we move beyond the automaticity of the obligatory "thanks" to practicing authentic gratitude with kids, peers, and the world? How can we unlock the power of gratitude to nurture relationships, improve well-being, and inspire learning? How can we empower our kids to be agents of change who make the world a better place? These are the questions that this book is designed to help you answer. Spoiler alert: there isn't just one correct answer. And before we get to the *how*, as well as to inspiring stories from other educators practicing gratitude, let's look at the *why* and the *what*.

Thankfully, education has become more focused on social-emotional learning (SEL) and serving the whole child. But what exactly is SEL, and why is it important? The Collaborative for Academic, Social, and Emotional Learning (CASEL), the US's leading organization in SEL in education, defines SEL as "an integral part of education and human development. SEL is the process through which all young people and adults acquire and apply the knowledge, skills, and attitudes to develop healthy identities, manage emotions and achieve personal and collective goals, feel and show empathy for others, establish and maintain supportive relationships, and make responsible and caring decisions."[1]

And while there is still work to be done to bring SEL into our learning spaces, as well as a lot of variation in approaches and levels of success from school to school and classroom to classroom, one thing is certain: For our learning communities to truly thrive and flourish, we must embrace the evidence that gratitude plays a significant role in relationships, well-being, and academic success. More specifically, practicing gratitude helps us improve in all five of CASEL's core SEL competencies:

- Self-Awareness
- Self-Management
- Social Awareness
- Relationship Skills
- Responsible Decision-Making

I hope that as you read this book, you find more evidence that it is time to make gratitude a priority for the sake of those we serve, as well as ourselves as educators (and parents). By strengthening our gratitude muscles, each of us can flourish socially, emotionally, and academically.

In the interest of full disclosure, practicing gratitude does not mean we will be joyful all the time. (And nothing makes you feel more like a fool than losing your cool about something insignificant in front of your family while writing a book on gratitude.) We must appreciate that what we call *negative emotions* (e.g., sadness, anger, disappointment) are part of the full human experience, and they do serve a purpose. Unpleasant is not the same as unnecessary. We need these emotions to guide us, serving as signals and signposts that help us stay safe—even alerting us when professional help may be necessary, especially when these intense and unpleasant feelings are pervasive and relentless. We don't want to suppress these feelings, but rather we want to acknowledge them and manage them. You might even leverage an emotion such as anger in competitive settings like sports or an academic debate.

In the book *Permission to Feel*, Marc Brackett, research psychologist and founding director of the Yale Center for Emotional Intelligence, offers an example of how negative emotions can help us. He explains that "anxiety narrows our attention and improves our focus on details. It makes us anticipate what could go wrong. That may not seem like a feeling we'd welcome, but it's a good frame of mind when we're performing tasks involving numbers, such as finances."[2]

An emotion might also have something to teach us. For example, researcher and storyteller Brené Brown says, "Regret is a fair but tough teacher."[3] When we make mistakes we regret, that unpleasantness, or even pain, tells us we don't want to experience this again and, hopefully, we reflect and learn from it.

In other words, all emotions exist for a reason, so the goal isn't to completely eliminate certain emotions. The goal is to regulate so that we don't have too many occurrences, we can avoid overreaction, and we don't stay in those negative emotions too long. This is something I'm getting better at, and it is something I will work continually to improve on each and every day. Personally, I don't even know how many meltdowns I (and those around me) have been spared thanks to a grateful disposition. Nor can I quantify the number of times that practicing gratitude has kept me from wallowing in despair.

Since the goal isn't to completely avoid the negative emotions, why do *you* want to cultivate authentic gratitude? The answer will vary from person to person and school to school. Perhaps you are focused on gratitude making a positive impact on learning. Maybe you see it as a way to improve relationships. Is overall well-being your goal? It could be all of the above. Really think about your *why* for gratitude, and take a moment to write or sketch it in the space provided. (If you have a digital version of this book, consider grabbing a piece of paper, opening your notes app, or recording a voice memo whenever you see these spaces.)

When I initially decided to write this book, I thought it would be relatively easy to explore a simple concept like gratitude. After all, I actively practice gratitude every day both personally and as an educator. Still, I quickly became overwhelmed with the nuance and complexity, and the fact that experts still have more to learn and don't always agree. Not to mention how our own individuality plays into all of this. Don't worry, I won't take you into the weeds with me. I read the latest science of gratitude books, listened to countless podcasts, and watched dozens of videos so you don't have to. Instead, this book will stay focused on what we know about gratitude, based on current research, and how we can bring those benefits into our education community. From there, you can select and adapt practices that are most effective for you and your learning community.

In fact, to honor your time, I *attempt* to use word economy and give you the critical content (the *why, what,* and *how*) in about one hundred pages. (If I fail, you won't be reading this, because the editors will have pulled it for accuracy, haha.) Regardless, there are resources at the end of the book offering you the opportunity to read, listen, and watch (like I did) to dig deeper as you continue on your own journey. But be warned: Jay Shetty, a former monk turned storyteller, calls gratitude "the world's most addictive drug."[4]

Another reason I'm focused on word economy is to make space for educators from around the globe to share how they experience and express gratitude with kids, peers, and the world. Stories are how we make meaning of the world, and stories of gratitude can be incredibly powerful. I hope they bring you as much joy as they brought me.

CHAPTER 1

What Is Gratitude?

> *Be thankful for what you have; you'll end up having more. If you concentrate on what you don't have, you will never, ever have enough.*
>
> —Oprah Winfrey

Before you read the definition that follows (seriously, no peeking), take a moment to think about what gratitude means to you. Even better, write it down. Think about a time that you experienced genuine gratitude. What was the gratitude for? Who was involved? How did you feel? Name the feelings. Did you do something in response to your feelings? I suggest you write or sketch it.

Dr. Robert Emmons, one of the world's leading experts on the science of gratitude, explains that gratitude "has been conceptualized as an emotion, a virtue, a moral sentiment, a motive, a coping response, a skill, and an attitude. It is all of these and more. Minimally, gratitude is an emotional response to a gift. It is the appreciation felt after one has been the beneficiary of an altruistic act."[1]

Furthermore, Dr. Emmons and Michael E. McCullough offer a widely accepted definition with gratitude as two parts:

1. "recognizing that one has obtained a positive outcome," and
2. "recognizing that there is an external source for this positive outcome."[2]

We don't just see the good, we also recognize that the efforts of outside forces (often other people) led to that positive outcome. Think about that in the context of our learning communities. We are better together!

As we look at our relationship with gratitude, through the lens of growth and development (from childhood to adolescence to adulthood) and our own continuing self-improvement as adults, it becomes evident that there is a spectrum of gratitude. Kids and adults have the capacity to evolve over time from simple reciprocity to developing a grateful disposition.

This is an important shift, as it moves us from experiencing gratitude as a fleeting emotion to a sustained disposition. It's more than "I feel grateful." It's "I am a grateful person." Gratitude becomes part of our identity, and it impacts how we experience and engage in everything.

To be clear, there are basic forms of gratitude that are part of the social contract. For example, if we drop a pen and someone picks it up for us, the expectation is that we say thank you to that person. We engage in simple reciprocity as polite members of society, and we want that to continue. However, gratitude has so much more to offer when we have a grateful disposition.

SPECTRUM OF GRATITUDE

simple
reciprocity

grateful
disposition

So how do we move from simple reciprocity to a grateful disposition? Here is the most concise answer I can give you, based on what I have learned from the leading experts and my own gratitude journey: Having a grateful disposition means that you practice gratitude with authenticity and specificity even in challenging times. Basically, we train our brains to reframe both the good and the bad in life. We don't take the good for granted, and we look for opportunities, lessons, or both in the bad. This does not mean we ignore the bad, especially when we find ourselves in a bad situation that we need to address. For example, if someone is consistently treating us poorly, we don't want to ignore the situation or force ourselves to find the good in them. We need to have a conversation letting them know that it isn't acceptable and remove ourselves from that relationship if necessary.

Knowing the importance of authenticity and specificity, we can be more thoughtful with our gratitude. In the book *The Gratitude Project*, Jeremy Adam Smith shares that "the richest thank-yous will acknowledge **intentions** (the pancakes you make when you see I'm hungry) and **costs** (you massage my feet after work, even when you're really tired), and they'll describe the **value** of the benefits received (you give me hugs when I'm sad so that I'll feel better)."[3] We will take a deeper dive into specific ways to practice gratitude in chapter 2, but we can immediately appreciate the power of acknowledging intentions, costs, and value.

I'm committed to being as transparent as possible when I share my journey and my relationship with gratitude, so I will start by saying that I struggle with indebtedness. I mean, I struggle deeply. I won't bore you with the source of all that struggle, but I will share how it manifests. When someone does something nice for me, I often feel guilt and an urgency to reciprocate (possibly even outdo their kindness). If someone pays me a compliment, I tend to deflect or downplay whatever the compliment was for. If I'm having lunch with someone and they offer to pick up the check, I might insist on getting it. (Even when my original plan was for us to split it.) In doing this, I rob the other person of the joy of gratitude and, knowing this, I don't feel great, either. I'm working on it, and I won't lie: this one's gonna take some time because this is part of my personal character.

Since I may not be the only one who struggles with this, I want to share some specific strategies I'm working on when I feel that indebtedness coming on:

- Savor the intentions, costs, and value: Pause to reflect on the gift received. Then, with authenticity and specificity, thank the person without one-upping their efforts.
- Pay it forward: Rather than deflecting or downplaying a compliment or a gesture, redirect that energy into prosocial behaviors like an act of kindness for a stranger.
- Share the compliment: There are times when we, as individuals, are celebrated for work that others contributed to. This is a great opportunity to gracefully accept the compliment and assure the person complimenting that you will also pass it on to your collaborators.

What Are the Benefits?

If we can find a way of becoming more positive in the present, then our brains work even more successfully. As we're able to work harder, faster, and more intelligently . . . dopamine, which floods your system when you're positive, has two functions. Not only does it make you happier, it turns on all of the learning centers in your brain.

—Shawn Achor

The Greater Good Science Center at UC Berkeley is dedicated to the scientific understanding of psychology, sociology, and the neuroscience of well-being. The center provides tons of practices, as well as resources on gratitude, and some of the research cited in this book comes from the center's work on social and emotional well-being. According to the research, actively practicing gratitude:

- helps us cope with stress
- regulates our emotions
- makes us happier
- improves our health
- nurtures relationships
- energizes learning

The Hedonic Treadmill and Happiness Chemicals

Let's geek out a little! When it comes to the science of happiness, studies show that we have a set point, or baseline, of happiness. The hedonic treadmill (aka hedonic adaptation) is the theory that even after major positive events, we tend to return to our set point relatively quickly. In other words, most of us are always a certain amount of happy, and even a glorious day at the beach or a dream vacation isn't gonna make a huge difference in how happy we are. We will just go back to a regular level of happiness soon. That may sound depressing, but there is good news. Gratitude keeps us at a higher level of happiness for longer for two reasons: (1) when we are intentionally grateful for the good in our lives, we maintain joy rather than taking things for granted, and (2) practicing gratitude releases two happiness chemicals, serotonin and dopamine. These two feel-good chemical messengers are neurotransmitters that promote a happy mood and positive feelings. (I did say I would geek out a little, so if you want more on this, see research cited in the back.) Here is where it gets really interesting: This is how we rewire our brains! By consistently and intentionally practicing gratitude, we are strengthening the neural pathways! According to research by Emmons, "People who regularly practice grateful thinking can increase their 'set point' for happiness by as much as 25 percent."[4] Who doesn't want to be 25 percent happier? Imagine what this could do for our learning communities!

There is plenty of science to back up the importance, as well as the benefits, of gratitude, but most people are convinced by their own experience and in a relatively short amount of time. Even after just a couple of weeks of intentionally practicing gratitude, most people notice a difference in the way they feel and act toward others. Give it a try every day for two weeks, and you will likely be a believer. As the saying goes, "It's not happy people who are grateful, it's grateful people who are happy."

Equifinality

As we start this gratitude journey, it is important to keep in mind that there is no recipe for practicing gratitude. In gratitude, as in all aspects of our lives, we see that a one-size-fits-all approach is not effective. Imagine going to a restaurant with one item on the menu, a movie theater with one movie playing, or a gym with one size weights for all the dumbbells. Enter one of my favorite words, *equifinality*. Merriam-Webster defines *equifinality* as the property of allowing or having the same effect or result from different events. Put another way, we can all get good results, but we don't have to do the exact same things to get there. There are people all over the world practicing gratitude personally and professionally, but there is no one way to do it.

Equifinality will be a recurring theme throughout this book, because we are all unique and dynamic individuals; therefore, what works for me to develop and maintain a grateful disposition may not work for you and vice versa. Our dispositions encompass our values, principles, and practices, and these are shaped by our culture, faith, family, friends, gender, genes, and more. That's a lot!

In *Atlas of the Heart*, Brené Brown provides us with the four Bs as a powerful way to think about all our emotions and experiences as layers of biology, biography, behavior, and backstory.[5] Here is how I apply the four Bs to explore the unique and dynamic way each of us experience and express gratitude:

→ Biology: How does gratitude manifest in our bodies? Why? (We can even think back to the *happiness chemicals* discussed earlier.)

→ Biography: How do our families and communities shape our gratefulness?

→ Behavior: How do we give and receive gratitude in our day-to-day lives? What does this look like?

→ Backstory: What is the context of our gratitude? What brought us to this way of being grateful?

In my own family, I watch my kids and how they are so different in everything, including how they experience and express gratitude. Kendall, eleven years old, is fiercely independent but never forgets to say thank you for what others do for her, no matter how small it is. She also can't help but show appreciation by doing something kind in return. Blake, eight years old, will give you the most heartfelt thank-you as his face lights up with appreciation. I know I'm biased, but I don't think you will find anyone more expressive in their delight.

I would love to take all the credit for the way Kendall and Blake are developing their grateful dispositions, but it isn't just families that shape our kids, and they have been blessed to have amazing teachers over the years to help. Their teachers have modeled showing gratitude by sharing their success at school via notes home, emails, text messages, and more. I'm also grateful that their teachers have allowed me to share what makes my kids special outside of school so that they can honor it in class as well. This nurtures the connection between school and home, which makes kids feel seen, heard, known, and valued.

One of my favorite things about writing this book is the opportunity to share other educators' stories of gratitude. I could not wait to hear what gratitude means to them, and I'm honored and thrilled to share this first story from Livia Chan, a head teacher in British Columbia, Canada, and someone who truly embodies a grateful disposition.

The Gift of Gratitude

by Livia Chan

**Head Teacher & Digital Content Coordinator
for the Teach Better Team
Burnaby, British Columbia, Canada**

Gratitude—a cultivated mindset that
Illuminates abundance and helps you
Find happiness as your heart and mind
Truly grow to experience even more gratitude.

Do you love epiphanies as much as I do? I have discovered simple truths that have changed my life. It stems from the idea that there are many gifts swirling all around us just waiting to be appreciated. The more I open my heart to feel, and the more I open my eyes to see possibilities, the greater my capacity to experience these as gifts.

One such gift is the gift of gratitude. It is truly remarkable. The more we dive into the practice of gratitude and expand what we are grateful for, the more abundant we will find it in our daily lives. Start with the little things we often take for granted. See them as gifts. There's something about receiving gifts that makes us feel grateful. When gratitude is cultivated in our hearts and minds, it grows. What we spend time on, give attention to, and nurture will continue to grow. As a result, our perspective on life changes. We evolve. As our gratitude evolves, life improves, too.

It is a choice to be grateful. When we choose to see our experiences, interactions, and anything in our lives through a lens of gratitude, what follows is happiness and hopefully joy. So open your heart and mind to see more things as gifts to be grateful for. Truly look around to find what brings you the greatest joy and start there.

One of the greatest epiphanies is how deeply grateful I am for the relationships I have. I used to take them for granted, thinking people will always be there for me, until one morning, twenty years ago, my beloved grandma never woke up. It was the biggest wake-up call. Since then, I've learned to see that relationships are truly gifts to value daily and to express my gratitude regularly, especially when it rests on my heart. No regrets. Never do I ever want to say again, I wish I had the opportunity to tell them how much they meant to me or how grateful I felt to have them in my life. The opportunity is there every day. Make every interaction count. It's that simple! Here's something I live by daily: in every interaction, we have an *opportunity* to intentionally *uplift* others through our kindness and gratitude to help make their day a brighter one.

How many times have you received kind words of genuine gratitude that brightened your day, warmed your heart, and put an instant smile across your face? Have you ever hugged the kind words you received? I have! That is the true gift of a grateful heart shared with yours. It is the gift of words.

Gratitude is meant to be shared. When you feel it, share it! When someone is placed in your heart or mind, there is a reason. It's the universe nudging you to reach out, show appreciation, and uplift them instantly. It's like packaging up sunshine and shipping it over in the form of words intentionally chosen. Trust that there is a ripple effect by reaching out to share your gratitude. They will remember how you made them feel . . . appreciated! It deepens your relationship too, which is key to your effectiveness as an educator.

Your specific words of gratitude can have such an impact on others to uplift them. But have you noticed how you feel uplifted as well? Showing kindness and gratitude are two of the best forms of self-care! To know that you brought joy to someone else's heart brings joy to yours.

Be the one who makes an impact through every interaction, but don't forget about yourself! Make time to be grateful for yourself and others, too. Having a strong appreciation for yourself helps you be whole for others you serve. You'll be amazed at the results for both.

You can make an impact and imprint on someone's heart by a simple expression of gratitude. Open your eyes to see possibilities. Possibilities will turn into opportunities. It's incredible how gratitude grows. The relationships I've built through gratitude have been truly life changing.

Model kindness and gratitude through every interaction, and then teach it to others. Imagine a world where we all will be blessed with joy in our hearts. The gift of gratitude is as much for you as it is for them! Happy gratitude gifting!

Livia's call to action inspires me to be even more intentional with every interaction and in all the micromoments we are fortunate to get with those around us, at school and at home. No interaction is too small to express gratitude. You never know the impact it could have.

Before we dive into the practical details of gratitude practices, please take a moment to imagine what would happen if you were to actively and intentionally practice gratitude every day for at least two weeks. This can be in the context of education or you personally practicing gratitude. What are your best hopes and your worst fears? What changes would you expect to see in your life both personally and professionally? You can write or sketch it in the space provided.

CHAPTER 2

Gratitude Practices

> *Look around, look around at how lucky we are to be alive right now!*
> —Lin-Manuel Miranda, *Hamilton: An American Musical*

When should we practice gratitude? In good times? In bad times? Yes. Who should we practice with? On our own? With others? Yes.

Gratitude in the Midst of Adversity

March of 2020 was a surreal time for many of us. We faced a global pandemic that seemed to knock the world off its axis. It forced us to face the fragility of life, and it stripped away many of the everyday things that we tend to take for granted. Laura Kelly Fanucci's poem "When This Is Over" captured this beautifully:

When this is over,
may we never again
take for granted
A handshake with a stranger
Full shelves at the store
Conversations with neighbors

A crowded theatre
Friday night out
The taste of communion
A routine checkup
The school rush each morning
Coffee with a friend
The stadium roaring
Each deep breath
A boring Tuesday
Life itself.
When this ends,
may we find
that we have become
more like the people
we wanted to be
we were called to be
we hoped to be
and may we stay
that way—better
for each other
because of the worst.[1]

I have shared this poem multiple times and in multiple places. I love how it compels us to appreciate the little things and how connected we are as people. It also compels us to confront the reality that our experiences during lockdown, such as food insecurity and isolation, were and still are an everyday occurrence for far too many people in this world, including some of the kids in our schools. Fanucci's poem doesn't ask us to ignore tragedy, but it does allow us to aspire for an even better future because of what we learned during this tragedy. It is an opportunity to reflect on the past as well as a lens for the present and the future.

In difficult times, I've tried it both ways—living with a grateful disposition *or* focusing on the negative things that I can't control. It's my experience that one feels much better than the other, offering me resilience and hope. It also gives me strength and a feeling of self-efficacy that empowers me to help others.

As educators during emergency remote teaching, many of us were able to stay connected with our learners, their families, and our colleagues to continue nurturing those relationships. Thanks to video conferencing, learning management systems, and other tools, we were able to both synchronously and asynchronously connect in meaningful ways. It was challenging in countless ways and far from ideal, but there were wins, such as "hearing" from kids who never raised their hands in class but used the chat feature to share their thoughts. Or having your internet drop and jumping back into the Zoom session to find that one of your students took over your lesson to keep the class going. And who could forget wearing sweatpants while teaching? (It didn't take me long to lean into that one!)

Tragedies like a global pandemic are filled with heartbreak and sadness, but they are also an opportunity to take a breath, be mindful of what we have, set an intention to never take things for granted again, and vow to be even better in the future.

I have practiced gratitude for years, but since March of 2020, I have tried to savor moments of joy, and I've been much more intentional in reflecting on the many reasons I have to be thankful. It is not an exaggeration to say that gratitude has helped me not only survive, but also thrive and flourish during difficult times. And I'm not alone.

Jennifer Evans, a nurse, wife of a fire chief, mother of two girls, and experienced Parent Teacher Student Association (PTSA) president, added another honorable title to that list in the fall of 2020—homeschool teacher. Now back at her neighborhood public school, Jennifer recalls how the simple practice of using a gratitude jar impacted her family during difficult times, and why they continue the practice even as a sense of normalcy returns.

From Groans to Gratitude

by Jennifer Evans

Nurse and Experienced Homeschool Teacher, Huntington Beach, California

It can be a grind. Groundhog Day, as it were. Morning alarm sounds. Take a deep breath. "Girls, wake up!" I'm prepared for the groans and resistance, and yet I find myself thinking, "Maybe today will be different. Maybe today I will be met with smiles, and the girls will hit the ground running, eager for new experiences, new knowledge." Again . . . nothing but groans. Therein lies the problem. We start our days with an attitude of resistance rather than gratitude. Gratitude that we have been given one more breath, one more day to start over, one more outing with friends and families, and one more day to learn! So, I face the challenge head on: teach my kids gratitude rather than groans.

Then we are dropped into the middle of a pandemic, and we distance our children from others, teach them to stay away, wash their hands incessantly, and not approach new friends at the park. Some, like myself, take the giant leap of faith and decide to homeschool my children. Kit Kat Academy opens its doors, and we start our very own home sweet homeschool. From mom to teacher overnight! The problem is that some days I, too, start with a groan. Until the day when a creative friend gave me a "gratitude jar." Gratitude? Huh! In the middle of this terrifying world, chaotic home, and unusual classroom, can we actually be grateful? Can we as family, as a class, as humans find the priceless positives in our lives? Surprisingly enough, my children answered the call with grace and gratitude and change happened in unexpected ways.

Lesson number one: teach gratitude. Lesson number two: practice gratitude. And lesson number three: celebrate that we as parents, siblings, students, and teachers are happier in our daily lives simply because we are grateful.

Using the gratitude jar became a ritual at the beginning of our school day. Start out with an emotion of gratitude. Take a card and write down what you are grateful for. Simple, right? As expected, it started out basic. "I am thankful for food." "I am thankful for my mom and dad." "I am thankful for my life." We talked a lot about being grateful, and we practiced gratitude in every corner of life—at the grocery store, at friends' homes, in the car, at our home, and with each other. Sometimes, it's as simple as saying thank you. And sometimes it is more pronounced.

As our gratitude practice evolved, it became part of our school mission. Be strong. Be kind. Be confident. Be grateful. It became part of who we are as humans. In essence, gratefulness became part of our own personal fabric, and the ability to express gratitude developed in surprising ways. Hearing Riley, then ten years old, say, "I am grateful for the strength to push through," or Madison, nine at the time, declare, "I am grateful for the happiness that everyone brings to me and all the beautiful nature in my life," naturally propelled us forward in a more positive direction. And you know what? As expressions of gratitude became a daily practice, I started to see change in my children. They woke up easier. They approached school with enthusiasm and excitement rather than that dreaded sigh. Their confidence soared, and the way they approached people became gentler. They viewed the world through grateful glasses and found something to appreciate in different people and difficult situations.

Who knew that this little jar would have such a dramatic impact on our lives? But it did. The simple act of being grateful changed our approach to life. It changed our approach to school. It changed us! It was astounding. It was rewarding. It was simply magical!

It seems that it is a paradox of life that in some of the darkest and most challenging times, we start to appreciate what we have and what is most important. And while some may struggle wondering if gratitude is possible and even appropriate in times of adversity, this is actually when we need our grateful disposition the most.

Gratitude for the Good in Life (and in Education)

No matter when you are reading this, if you, at this very moment, turn on the news, grab a newspaper, or go to a news website, what is the headline? Is it good news or bad news? Look at the other stories. What is the ratio of positive to negative information? Is it more positive or more negative? I bet I know. And when education makes the headlines, is it more often positive or negative?

As humans, we are wired with a negativity bias, meaning that even in the best of times, we notice the negative exponentially more, and it can haunt us. Considered an adaptive evolutionary function, negativity bias served a critical purpose thousands of years ago, helping our ancestors make choices to survive.[2] And, as discussed in the introduction, negative emotions also serve a purpose and can help keep us safe, but negativity bias can have us overwhelmingly focused on the negative in unproductive ways. Consider this: As an educator, how many times have things gone well in lessons and in interactions with learners, families, and colleagues? Countless times, right? Yet, when things don't go well, it is all we think about! The explanation of a concept that didn't help kids, the misunderstanding with a peer, even that joke that didn't land. (It was hilarious, by the way!) Yes, this can motivate us to continuously improve, but we also need ways to regulate so it is productive, not destructive. Practicing gratitude can help us amplify the positive and find more balance.

Given the constant barrage of negativity and humans' propensity to see the bad, how can we see the good and be grateful for it? We can start by intentionally looking for it and appreciating it. In his TED Talk "Is the World Getting Better or Worse? A Look at the Numbers," Steven Pinker shares his analysis of the data on homicide, war, poverty, pollution, and more compared to thirty years prior. I encourage you to watch the talk, so I won't give it all away, but here's a hint: you may be pleasantly surprised (and dare I say grateful?) by our progress. According to Pinker, "We will never have a perfect world, and it would be dangerous to seek one. But there's no limit to the betterments we can attain if we continue to apply knowledge to enhance human flourishing."[3] Can't we say the same about education? There is so much good in our profession and our kids that there is no limit to what we can achieve, if we continue to focus on thriving and flourishing! To me, Pinker's talk is an inspiring public expression of gratitude for our continuing progress and a call to action to celebrate it.

THERE IS SO MUCH GOOD IN OUR PROFESSION AND OUR KIDS THAT THERE IS NO LIMIT TO WHAT WE CAN ACHIEVE, IF WE CONTINUE TO FOCUS ON THRIVING AND FLOURISHING!

Navigating Negativity Bias in Education

Education is a profession that tends to attract highly altruistic people who want to be the very best they can be and who work tirelessly to do so. The downside is that this can lead to being extra critical of ourselves and to struggles with practicing self-care. Naomi Toland, a head teacher in Auckland, New Zealand, and founder of Empathetic Educators, is a dedicated teacher who cares deeply about others. She leads with empathy and promotes "empathy not at the expense of ourselves." Here is how Naomi connects gratitude to her work as an empathetic educator.

Empathy for Ourselves through Gratitude

by Naomi Toland

Head Teacher
Auckland, New Zealand

How we see the world impacts how we experience it. During challenging times especially, our inner thoughts can have a significant impact on our perspective and, in turn, how we choose to deal with it.

Having empathy for ourselves and weaving that into our day-to-day lives can help us take control of our thoughts and actions. One way to do this is through gratitude. Gratitude can help us shift from having a negative script in our minds, spiraling down and out of control, to an optimistic script, working to help us build our way back up. As Madhuleena Roy Chowdhury so elegantly put it, "By merely acknowledging and appreciating the little things in life, we can rewire the brain to deal with the present circumstances with more awareness and broader perception."[4]

In my first year of teaching, my mind began to spiral out of control. I was continually attacking myself for every single mistake I made, expecting myself to be this amazing teacher with no flaws, instead of accepting that I was in the early years of my craft so the only way to learn was by trying new things, making mistakes, and learning from them. This negative self-talk began to take a toll on me physically, and I began to get migraines on a weekly basis, something I had never had before. That was when I realized something had to change, something had to give. I seriously considered leaving the profession I had wanted to join since I was five years old. How could that be?

So instead of leaving, I decided to start learning about what was going on inside of my head and start to empathize with and understand myself and those around me. Why were my thoughts changing in such a way? Why was I feeling like a failure all of the time? Why was I feeling one way on the inside but showing a different face on the outside?

This is when I started looking at ways to grow my mental strength. Just like going to the gym to train my body, I started going to the mental gym to train my brain. One of the methods I used was practicing gratitude.

Saying "I have to do" locks us into our thoughts, telling ourselves we must do something as an obligation. I started to shift my inner voice to say "I get to do." This allowed me to appreciate and feel gratitude for all the things I get to do in the day, and acknowledging this started to rewire my brain to see things in a different light.

Now, I am not saying it worked every time. Sometimes after having a car crash of a lesson, followed by a challenging parent conversation, followed by an extended after-school team meeting, it might have been hard to say "I get to do this." But even on those days, I tried to remind myself "I get to learn and try again tomorrow in my lesson; I get to speak with a parent about how we can try to move forward together to help their child; I get to sit in a safe building, and I get to go home after this meeting and make dinner."

Practicing gratitude helped me get out of my head for a while and look at things from a different angle and to think about my current situation from a different perspective—not to minimize or undervalue my experience, just to see if there might be a different path I could choose to take. The more I did this, the more it helped me take stock, let me focus on what I do have, instead of what I don't have, and move forward from there.

> In a world of stimulation and information, it can be tricky to take control of our thoughts and actions, but my own life experiences have made me realize the importance of holding myself and others accountable and creating systems that help us establish safe, engaging environments that allow all to flourish.

Getting Started

> *When I started counting my blessings, my whole life turned around.*
>
> —Willie Nelson

I often speak and write about inquiry-based learning. I encourage kids to explore content on their own and with their peers to construct knowledge, rather than waiting for me, the teacher, to have all the answers. I suggest the same with gratitude. However, when it comes to practices within the SEL realm, it is understandable that some of us might feel better trying things on our own, or with friends and family, before bringing them into our learning community. You might also consider finding a gratitude mentor. This could be someone you know or a public figure who you think embodies gratitude. Watch what they do to experience and express gratitude. Could you use or adapt some of their strategies?

You may want to start by auditing how grateful you are. Based on the work of psychologists Mitchel Adler and Nancy Fagley, the Greater Good Science Center at UC Berkeley has developed a quick fifteen-question gratitude quiz available at greatergood.berkeley.edu.[5] The quiz focuses on how you experience gratitude. It is also important to think about how you *express* gratitude. Even if that mainly consists of a sincere thank-you to a stranger holding a door open for you. Personally, I find that when I reflect on who I show gratitude toward, I realize that I never forget to thank that stranger holding the door for me, yet I often forget to thank my husband for taking the trash out, a task I hate to do! I'm working on it, and I've found that the saying "better late than never" applies here. In our schools and homes, we often miss opportunities to show gratitude to those who do the most for us. When we do this, we are withholding a gift that can have very positive effects on the recipient. But we can change that! What follows in this chapter are a variety of practices you can try, and the remaining chapters will give specific examples of the practices in action with kids, peers, and the world!

Options for Everyone

Along with a gratitude self-assessment, the Greater Good Science Center has curated a treasure trove of gratitude practices, and I encourage you to visit their Greater Good in Action website at ggia.berkeley.edu to search for more, but here are some key practices to get you started.

Gratitude Journals

Without question, one of the most widely used gratitude practices is the gratitude journal, and with good reason. In *The Gratitude Project*, the authors explain that "research suggests translating thoughts into concrete language makes us more aware of them, deepening their emotional impact."[6] Essentially, we are telling ourselves the story of who and what we are grateful for. If that doesn't convince you, maybe Oprah will. In season 2, episode 206 of *Oprah's Lifeclass*, Oprah shares that she has been using a gratitude journal for many years, and it is the single most important thing she's ever done.[7] Now that's an endorsement!

You do not need a fancy gratitude journal. You can even use a blank journal, go digital, or choose analog. I often joke that it's like I'm allergic to paper because I almost always prefer a digital copy of things, but this is one of those times that I prefer to go with old-fashioned pen and paper. Some people make lists and some like to write a narrative. As discussed in chapter 1, equifinality is a reality. There are different paths for different people. You may even want to revisit Brené Brown's four Bs—biology, biography, behavior, and backstory—as you consider your options.

Regardless of how you choose to journal, the goal of the practice is to remember someone or something that you are grateful for—an event, experience, person, or thing. Be as specific as possible on the details, name the feelings, and relish the good emotions associated. Ideally, you also feel compelled to do something to express gratitude toward others. (This can also bring you joy!)

Now, maybe you have already tried a gratitude journal, or you know someone who has, but writing about the people and things you (or they) are grateful for didn't have the positive outcomes you would expect. This is another opportunity to appreciate that we are all unique and dynamic.

Neuroscience might also offer an explanation for why traditional gratitude journals don't work for everyone. In November 2021, Dr. Andrew Huberman, a Stanford neurobiology professor, released episode 47 of the *Huberman Lab* podcast, "The Science of Gratitude & How to Build a Gratitude Practice."[8] In this episode, he explains that the recent scientific literature on gratitude found that the most effective gratitude practices must involve story (a narrative) and the receiving (not giving) of genuine gratitude.[9] Hmm, well, this sounds quite a bit tougher than writing about what we are grateful for, right? It doesn't have to be. In fact, you might find this an easier approach.

Here is the protocol Dr. Huberman suggests:

- Find a story of genuine gratitude that is meaningful, compelling, or moving to you.
  - Reflect deeply on a time when someone was thankful for something you did, or think about the story and emotional experience of someone else receiving help. (Amazingly, as humans we can experience positive feelings even if it wasn't our story!)
- Think about how you felt receiving that gratitude or how the person who was helped felt.
- List out the struggle, the help, and the emotional impact on you, so you can quickly refer back to this story for future practice.

The best part is, you don't need a new story each time. You can come back to your notes on this narrative and repeat the protocol, taking just a moment to deeply reflect on the highlights of the story and its impact.

To be clear, there is significant research, not to mention overwhelming anecdotal reporting, that supports traditional gratitude practices focused on *expressing* gratitude. The protocol Huberman is suggesting is focused on *experiencing* gratitude, and it is based on what brain imaging shows to yield the greatest results during specific scientific experiments. I believe we need to be open to evolving our gratitude practices, while also honoring what we know works best for us as individuals.

Gratitude Journals in Education

Outside of education, journals are often thought of as something personal and private like a diary. We want kids to feel comfortable writing whatever they are grateful for in their journals, and it is understandable that not everything that goes in there should be shared with peers, or even their teacher. However, when we set aside class time to journal for gratitude, I recommend asking learners to include at least one thing that they are comfortable sharing with others. This allows us, as teachers, to make room for everyone to express their gratitude without causing anxiety. Psychological safety is important for kids and adults, which is why I do the same thing when working with adult learners.

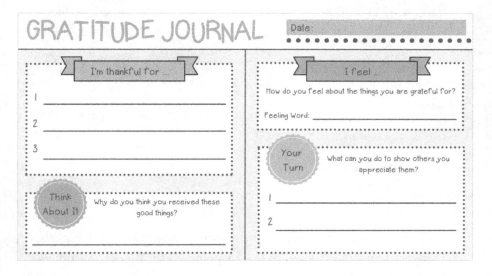

Megan Venezia, an SEL/Behavior Support TOSA (teacher on special assignment) in Tustin, CA, shares how she uses gratitude journals with kids: "The gratitude journal serves as a weekly reflection for each student. Students are encouraged to think about positive experiences that occurred during the week and document these experiences in their gratitude journals. (Students complete the activity using a digital slides template.) After individual reflections, the students gather in a closing circle to share and express their gratitude. This practice helps students to strengthen their social and emotional competencies as well as build a strong classroom community."

As described by Megan, her gratitude practice with learners involves both experiencing and expressing gratitude. Connecting this to Dr. Huberman's protocol, even if someone doesn't feel the full benefits of gratitude when they reflect on and share what they are grateful for, the sharing of these stories allows the entire community to observe and feel through others' stories of gratitude.

Avoiding Fatigue

Gratitude fatigue is a real possibility. We pull out our gratitude journals, ready to capture three things, and we maybe list something like:

1. my family
2. my students
3. my health

The next day, ready to dive back into that journal (perhaps after a rough day at work) and the list is:

1. my family
2. my friends
3. my health

On day three, here we go again, but today my kids didn't make their beds and didn't like the meal I prepared for dinner, so today's list includes:

1. my friends
2. my students
3. my health

You get the idea. This no longer feels like a gratitude practice; it feels more like a routine that lacks deep reflection, authenticity, and specificity. And side note, there isn't a definitive answer on how often we should write in our gratitude journals. Some swear that it has to be daily. Some say daily is too much, and it loses its impact. Research supports positive impact when journaling as few as two to three times a week. Regardless of frequency, the best way that I have found to keep it fresh is to pick themes for each entry. Here are some themes that I learned using Habit Nest's *The Gratitude Sidekick Journal* (and these themes are still in high rotation in my journal):

- Everyday things
- Relationships

- Coincidences
- Work
- Nature
- Experiences
- Adversity

Sometimes I get even more specific. For example, instead of *relationships*, I focus specifically on my own children or even one child. For *work*, I might home in on a specific collaboration or project that has been meaningful as I continue to learn and evolve. And thinking back to Dr. Huberman's suggested protocol for having a story of receiving or observing gratitude, there are actually benefits to returning to the same narrative when it comes to wiring (or rewiring) the brain. In other words, using the same story makes the brain more efficient in recognizing gratitude and retrieving those good feelings.

Note: If a gratitude journal was the perfect format for everyone, I would stop here, but it isn't. If you try it and you don't find it effective, please don't give up on gratitude. There are plenty of other practices to choose from!

Savoring Walks

We often think of savoring in the context of food and the ability to completely enjoy what we are eating or drinking. One of my favorite lines in Chris Van Allsburg's children's book *The Polar Express* is "we drank hot cocoa as thick and rich as melted chocolate bars." Even though it is only one line, I get the sense that the character truly appreciated how delicious and special the experience was. Savoring is really about the ability to enjoy anything fully. It is about being mindful of the experience and, more specifically, the internal or external stimuli that are responsible for the positive feelings we are experiencing.

This is a twenty-minute practice that helps us tune into our sense of wonder to truly notice and appreciate the good around us. If you have trouble imagining going outside for a walk and appreciating everything around you, I encourage you to pause here and watch Louie Schwartzberg's "Nature. Beauty. Gratitude." talk at TEDxSF.[10] His breathtaking time-lapse photography, accompanied by wise words from Benedictine monk Brother David Steindl-Rast, empower us to savor the sights, sounds, smells, or other sensations we often neglect. Here is an excerpt from the video's transcript to give you an idea of how Brother David lives gratefully:

> Begin by opening your eyes and be surprised that you have eyes you can open. That incredible array of colors that is constantly offered to us for pure enjoyment.
>
> Look at the sky. We so rarely look at the sky. We so rarely note how different it is from moment to moment, with clouds coming and going. We just think of the weather. And even of the weather, we don't think of all the many nuances of weather. We just think of good weather and bad weather.
>
> This day, right now, has unique weather, maybe a kind that will never exactly in that form come again. The formation of clouds in the sky will never be the same that is right now. Open your eyes. Look at that.

As you may have guessed, savoring isn't limited to walks or food. We can create savoring rituals by honoring even the smallest everyday moments like prolonging the joy of our first cup of coffee, staring at the sunrise or sunset, listening to our favorite music, cooking a yummy meal from scratch, and much more. When we get in the practice of savoring, we train our brains to be present and grateful.

WE CAN CREATE SAVORING RITUALS BY HONORING EVEN THE SMALLEST EVERYDAY MOMENTS LIKE PROLONGING THE JOY OF OUR FIRST CUP OF COFFEE, STARING AT THE SUNRISE OR SUNSET, LISTENING TO OUR FAVORITE MUSIC, COOKING A YUMMY MEAL FROM SCRATCH, AND MUCH MORE. WHEN WE GET IN THE PRACTICE OF SAVORING, WE TRAIN OUR BRAINS TO BE PRESENT AND GRATEFUL.

Savoring Walks in Education

We tend to spend the vast majority of our time learning inside. Why not take learning outside? A savoring walk is a great brain break (for kids and adults), and it could also serve as a prewriting or science activity allowing learners to observe nature and their surroundings, while noticing all the wonderful details. You can even offer prompts like "watch an ant for one full minute and notice how it moves," "watch the flight of a bird soaring above," and "find a cloud and imagine riding on it as it glides across the sky." Kids can take a notepad with them to capture their thoughts or freewrite when they return. They could also take a device and capture photos to reference later (as long as the devices don't become a distraction). Bonus: asking learners to share their observations can help us, as adults, rediscover the world through a child's eyes.

Counterfactual Thinking: Mental Subtraction

We often lament about comparison hangovers induced by social media but, even before social media existed, we had other media helping us feel bad about ourselves. Media of all kinds, from magazines and billboards to TV, are filled with aspirational messaging to catch our attention and entice us to make purchases in the hope that it will lead to happiness. The reality is that any time we do upward comparisons or compare ourselves to highly edited versions of people, gratitude is not likely the feeling that will overwhelm us. Consider this quote from author Regina Brett: "If we all threw our problems in a pile and saw everyone else's, we'd grab ours back."[11]

What if we were to move away from comparing ourselves and our circumstances to others? What if, instead, we were to take our current reality and compare it to a far less desirable scenario for ourselves? I'll go first and share an abbreviated version of my own mental subtraction here.

Example of Mental Subtraction

Positive Event: A requirement for earning my bachelor's degree in psychology was to do field work and, by chance, I ended up working at a school for learners with special needs.

If I had never volunteered at that school, I wouldn't have . . .

- worked with kids and realized that I wanted to be a teacher
- focused on learning about innovative ways to support and empower ALL learners
- worked with my colleagues who also became lifelong friends
- been given leadership opportunities in my school and later in my district
- had the courage to become an author and a podcaster
- enjoyed the opportunity to connect with other educators all around the world as a consultant

Most importantly, if I hadn't volunteered at that school, I might not have spent the last twenty-five years in a career that gives me purpose. Even as I write this, I realize what an important event that was, and I am overwhelmed with gratitude that my field work sent me down this path.

I suggest that you take a moment and try this yourself. Think of a positive in your life. It can be an event or a relationship. Deeply reflect on why this is so important to you. Now imagine your life without that event or person. Again, take the time to deeply reflect on the circumstances and the ripple effects. We often don't appreciate what we have until we imagine how different life could have been.

WE OFTEN DON'T APPRECIATE WHAT WE HAVE UNTIL WE IMAGINE HOW DIFFERENT LIFE COULD HAVE BEEN.

Counterfactual Thinking in Education

Entitlement is in opposition to gratitude, and I find it an interesting activity to brainstorm all the simple pleasures we experience in schools today that didn't exist for other generations and, sadly, are still not available in underserved communities. For example, clean water in the drinking fountains, plumbing that works, heat and air conditioning, Wi-Fi, internet, devices, etc. Using mental subtraction with students is an exercise in empathy and an opportunity to appreciate what we have in our learning environment.

Even More Ways to Add Variety to Gratitude Practices

- Do affirmations
- Make a *Three Things* list, and add a new word in front of *things*. For example, *Three Funny Things, Three Kind Things,* or *Three Awe-Inspiring Things*.
- Meditate
- Keep a gratitude rock in your pocket or wear something (e.g., a specific bracelet) as a physical reminder to pause and experience and express gratitude.
- Write a gratitude letter and personally deliver it and, if the recipient would appreciate it, read it to them.
- Start your day with a gratitude email to a peer. (Tara Martin, who you will meet later in the book, does this regularly and she finds it highly effective!)
- End your work day with a positive call to a student's family.

- Invite a friend or a family member to practice gratitude with you. Gratitude is personal, but it doesn't have to be a solo act, and sharing our stories of gratitude is mutually beneficial.

Notice-Think-Feel-Do

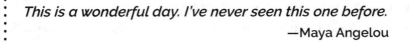

This is a wonderful day. I've never seen this one before.
—Maya Angelou

There will be more gratitude practices and stories shared throughout this book, but first consider how essential it is that, whatever practice we choose (for ourselves and for our learners), it must be done with intention. Notice-think-feel-do are the four essential components of the gratitude experience identified by psychologist Andrea Hussong and her team. Based on the scientific literature and conversations with parents, they've come to think about gratitude as an experience that has four parts:

- What we *notice* in our lives for which we can be grateful
- How we *think* about why we have been given those things
- How we *feel* about the things we have been given
- What we *do* to express appreciation in turn[12]

When we express our feelings of gratitude, it is crucial that we are genuine and as specific as possible. Just like when we provide learners feedback on their work, a simple "great job" doesn't offer much. In expressing gratitude (and feedback), we need to dig deep to show we truly recognize and value what they have given us.

IN EXPRESSING GRATITUDE (AND FEEDBACK), WE NEED TO DIG DEEP TO SHOW WE TRULY RECOGNIZE AND VALUE WHAT THEY HAVE GIVEN US.

Why not give it a try right now? Think of one thing you are grateful for and really process through all of the notice-think-feel-do questions and record your responses. You can write or sketch it in the space provided.

NOTICE

THINK

FEEL

DO

"Life moves pretty fast. If you don't stop and look around once in a while, you could miss it," is a famous line from the movie *Ferris Bueller's Day Off*, so it makes sense that the first step is to *notice*. I make it a personal challenge to notice and appreciate even the smallest of wins, which reminds me of Admiral McRaven's 2014 commencement speech at The University of Texas at Austin.[13] His inspiring speech has nearly four million views and is filled with words of wisdom. Most surprisingly, he spends time sharing why he thinks it is so important to make your bed every morning. He explains:

> If you make your bed every morning, you will have accomplished the first task of the day. It will give you a small sense of pride, and it will encourage you to do another task and another and another and, by the end of the day, that one task completed will have turned into many tasks completed. Making your bed will also reinforce the fact that the little things in life matter. If you can't do the little things right, you'll never be able to do the big things right. And if by chance you have a miserable day, you will come home to a bed that is made, that you made, and a made bed gives you encouragement that tomorrow will be better. So if you want to change the world, start off by making your bed.

Thank you for this powerful advice and for encouraging us to be grateful for even the tiniest victories, Admiral McRaven.

Building Gratitude Habits

A lot of people think what they need is intensity, but what they really need is consistency.
—James Clear

I often think about my aspirational self vs. my actual self. For example, my aspirational self recites Maya Angelou poems to my children every night, while cooking a homemade dinner from scratch. My actual self might order takeout while my kids watch their iPads, so I can catch up on work. (Not every night, but it happens.) The problem is that aspiring to be something isn't enough. We need to know our *why*, analyze what we need to work on, and establish rituals and routines to stay focused and avoid fatigue.

Rituals and routines are essential for me, both personally and professionally. Personally, the number of homemade meals my family eats every week has room for improvement, but we have bedtime rituals that are nonnegotiable to ensure we read together, truly connect, and practice gratitude every single day.

Professionally, I use the three SEL signature practices from CASEL whenever I work with kids or adults:

- Welcoming inclusion activities
- Engaging strategies
- Optimistic closure[14]

We can use the signature practices to intentionally and explicitly weave SEL into the fabric of our everyday learning. As shared in the introduction, gratitude is connected to all of CASEL's five core SEL competencies:

- Self-Awareness
- Self-Management
- Social Awareness
- Relationship Skills
- Responsible Decision-Making

And while the signature practices are not specific to gratitude, I like to connect one of them to gratitude. For example, in a welcoming inclusion activity, I might say, "List three things you are grateful for, and make sure to include at least one that you are comfortable sharing with the group." Then we go around the room (preferably standing or sitting in a circle) to share our experiences. If meeting via videoconference (e.g., Zoom or Google Meet), I have everyone use the chat. Every voice should be heard either out loud or via text.

As I plan, I think about where a gratitude practice would be most appropriate and helpful. It is highly unlikely that all three of the signature practices will be directly tied to gratitude (it is possible to overdo it), but the important thing is that I'm in the habit of using the signature practices, so I don't forget to make time for our community of learners to practice gratitude.

Since I like to minimize the gap between my aspirational self and my actual self (both personally and professionally), I start by giving myself realistic goals. For example, an unrealistic goal would be: I will practice gratitude at the top of every hour during waking hours seven days a week. We know how this is gonna go—I will fail! Let's try a realistic goal: I will practice gratitude once a day.

OK, that's better, but it still has a long way to go. As Carol Dweck shares in her seminal book *Mindset*, "Research by Peter Gollwitzer and his colleagues shows that vowing, even intense vowing, is often useless. The next day comes and the next day goes."[15] Instead, think about your gratitude practice in vivid detail:

- Who will you do this practice with?

    - You don't need to do this with someone else, and you may prefer to do this solo, especially at first. However, doing the practice with students, peers, friends, or family can hold you accountable (think of it as a commitment device), and you can keep each other motivated. You also get the benefit of hearing other stories of gratitude when you do your practice with others, which will most likely amplify the positive effects.

- What practice will you focus on?

- Gratitude journals are very popular, but they aren't right for everyone. If the practices shared so far don't resonate, hang tight. There are even more gratitude practices to choose from in the chapters that follow.

- When will you do your practice?

  - Could you do this first thing in the morning? Okay, before you stop reading this book thinking this is being written by a *morning person*, rest assured it is not! At all. You don't need to focus on the start of your day. Mornings do set the tone for our entire day, but really any time of day works!

  - If you are struggling to think of a way to squeeze the time in, think about the habits you currently practice that don't promote your physical, intellectual, spiritual, or emotional well-being and how you could remove, or at least delay, those. For example, waking up and checking messages on our phones while lying in bed is a habit that many of us have, but it can lead to losing track of time and making us late. Plus, one unpleasant message could shift our moods to the negative—not a great way to start the day.

  - Regardless of when you do your practice, how will you remember to do it? Could you dedicate space for it in your planner? Maybe place a note in a highly visible spot in your classroom or office so you see it first thing in the morning? My preference is to set a recurring reminder on my phone. Note: The reminders app on my phone is the only thing that I allow notifications from. I'm occasionally nagged by my social media apps to turn notifications on so I "don't miss anything" but that's a hard no! I train my technology to help me make good choices. Do you have tricks for minimizing the nagging from your devices?

For instance, maybe you keep your phone out of your bedroom at night?

- Where will the practice happen?

  - Will this take place in a classroom or staff room?
  - Could we go outside and stand in a circle?
  - Do you need a quiet space for deep reflection?

- How will you do it?

  - Visualize it. Play that *mind-movie* in your head so that you see yourself engaged in the practice. Here comes an important part: now actually write it down by making a list of the steps that need to happen, so you have a detailed plan.

The first week could be the hardest, but it will get easier over time and, eventually, you will get into a gratitude habit and reminders won't be necessary. Even better, these habits will lead to gratitude as a deep moral value and a grateful disposition. You can do it!

CHAPTER 3

Gratitude with Kids

> *We do not believe in ourselves until someone reveals that deep inside us something is valuable, worth listening to, worthy of our trust . . . Once we believe in ourselves we can risk curiosity, wonder, spontaneous delight or any experience that reveals the human spirit.*
>
> —E. E. Cummings

First, Gratitude for Kids

The best way to change someone else's behavior is to change our own behavior first. Before we focus on ways to make our learners grateful, how can we be grateful for our learners? Truth: we can't make grateful kids and cultivate a culture of authentic gratitude if we aren't modeling gratitude ourselves.

Think about a classroom or an online learning space that you have been in recently. It can be your own or one that you visited as an instructional coach, administrator, etc. Scan the space and see all of those wonderful faces. Think about all the things you can thank them for: coming to school, actively engaging in learning, offering a warm smile, helping others, and so much more. You continue scanning the room, and then you get to that one kid. This kid challenges you. Maybe they can't sit still, they can't stop talking, they show up late, they don't turn in assignments, or all of the above. What if this kid needs your gratitude more than you can imagine? What if this kid really needs to feel seen, heard, and genuinely appreciated? Often, the kids who challenge us the most are the ones who need us the most.

OFTEN, THE KIDS WHO CHALLENGE US THE MOST ARE THE ONES WHO NEED US THE MOST.

We know that gratitude improves relationships and, from a behavior modification perspective, we know that positive feedback is a highly effective way to reinforce the positive behaviors we want to see in our learning communities. I certainly don't remember everything from earning my psychology degree, but I will never forget learning that we should recognize positive behavior six times more than we recognize negative behavior. In other words, I should acknowledge a kid doing six things right for every one time I correct them.

Others may use a slightly different ratio. For example, maybe the praise-to-correction ratio is five to one. The point is, we overwhelmingly express appreciation for the good and correct as little as possible. Obviously, if there is a safety issue or an impact on other learners, we address it, but do we really need to call out every minor issue? No, we don't, and doing so usually does more to damage relationships than to change behavior.

At the time, I didn't realize I would become an educator, so I probably held on to this information to use when I became a parent and, wow, has it been a game changer in both roles! I won't pretend that using this ratio is easy, but it is very effective and very rewarding. It also promotes a culture of gratitude and diminishes resentment.

You may be wondering about the difference between praise and gratitude. (I did!) Gratitude is about recognizing the good and acknowledging its source. Ideally, we express our gratitude for the good in others, and one way to do that is praise. While neither should be done with the expectation of reciprocation, I find that both praise and gratitude are highly contagious.

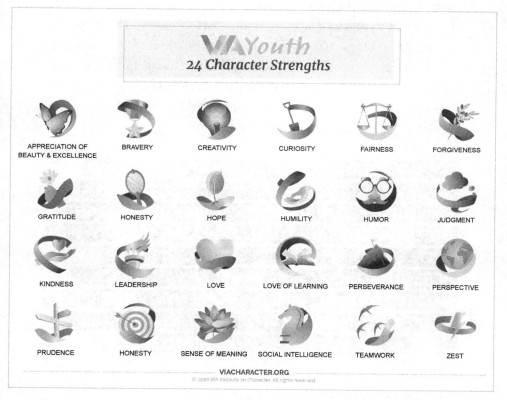

Figure 1 © Copyright 2004-2021, VIA Institute on Character.
All Rights Reserved. Used with Permission.

For an asset-based approach to identifying the positives in each child, consider using the VIA Survey of Character Strengths available at viacharacter.org. This is a great tool to find ways to be grateful for everyone, especially the ones who challenge us the most. And we all know that people do challenge us—personalities clash and some people just push our buttons. This is true of both adults and kids. But it's important to recognize that if we are struggling to identify any strengths in a child, this probably says more about us and our mental state than about the child. When I reflect on my biggest struggles with personalities, I can almost always trace it back to an issue I had with feeling entitled to respect (sometimes when I had yet to earn it) or being in a difficult place in my life. Reflect on what behaviors or personality traits push your buttons. Being conscious of these will help you find ways to navigate the more difficult relationships. We have to really challenge ourselves to find the good in each and every one of the precious kids we have been entrusted to serve, and we need to make sure they know we see the good in them.

IT'S IMPORTANT TO RECOGNIZE THAT IF WE ARE STRUGGLING TO IDENTIFY ANY STRENGTHS IN A CHILD, THIS PROBABLY SAYS MORE ABOUT US AND OUR MENTAL STATE THAN ABOUT THE CHILD. WHEN I REFLECT ON MY BIGGEST STRUGGLES WITH PERSONALITIES, I CAN ALMOST ALWAYS TRACE IT BACK TO AN ISSUE I HAD WITH FEELING ENTITLED TO RESPECT (SOMETIMES WHEN I HAD YET TO EARN IT) OR BEING IN A DIFFICULT PLACE IN MY LIFE.

Stories of Gratitude for Kids

Dr. Katie Novak is an internationally recognized expert in Universal Design for Learning (UDL) as well as an educator, author, proud momma of four, runner, and self-proclaimed lover of red heels. In this heartfelt story, you'll hear how Katie experienced gratitude when she was a kid in school.

Threads of Gratitude: A Legacy

by Katie Novak

Educator, Author, and Consultant
Groton, Massachusetts

My *mémère* was a seamstress.

As children, my sister and I sat by her sewing machine with remnants of fabric on our laps, waiting for our turn to create clothes for our stuffed animals. I remember sitting on Mémère's lap as she steadied my fingers so I could push fabric through the sewing machine. To this day, I am mesmerized by how thread spooling from the top of the machine and through the needle captures the thread from the bobbin beneath to make a beautiful and tight stitch.

As I think back on my journey in education, the threads that stitch my experiences together include moments of gratitude. I am grateful for the teachers and opportunities I had, but I am also keenly aware of the moments when teachers shared that they were grateful for me. Me, a kid! And these experiences remind me that it is not enough to look in a single direction to share our thanks and gratitude but to look everywhere around us.

In middle school, Ms. Dunlop, my English teacher, asked my parents if she could take me out for ice cream. She told my mom that she wanted to thank me, because she always knew that she could partner me with anyone. I knew that I wasn't the best student (Cs get degrees!), but I was kind, and I prided myself on that. Mom and Dad always told me being kind was more important than grades and having a teacher affirm that made me feel seen.

I ordered mint chocolate chip ice cream on a sugar cone at Dot's Dairy Bar. We sat outside on a picnic table and talked about our favorite books.

In grade eight, I was a homeroom representative for the student council. Every week I attended meetings and presented the news to my class. At the end of the year, Mrs. Ryan surprised me with a gift. She bought me a pair of jean shorts and had the whole class sign a card thanking me for being the student council rep. Everyone clapped and I wore those jean shorts pretty much every day for the rest of the year.

I made sure to weave this thread of gratitude into my own practice with learners when I became a teacher. With students, I scheduled one-to-one meetings to share how grateful I was for their creativity, their work ethic, their kindness, or their sass! I scheduled positive phone calls home and sometimes surprised my classes with hot chocolate bars with marshmallows and whipped cream. This wasn't an external reward they had to earn, but I did it because after thirty years, I remember the taste of that mint chocolate ice cream. In hindsight, I didn't do this enough and, if I could go back, I would certainly do more.

As educators, we are often thankful for exceptional leaders, supportive parents, and colleagues who hold us up, but looking at the students we serve, being grateful for them, and sharing those feelings is more powerful than you could imagine.

The lesson here is this: Gratitude doesn't come from a single thread. Like our mémère taught us with her sewing machine, a second thread is required to form a tight bond. And as grateful as I am for my own teachers, I am deeply grateful for my students and if I could, there would be an ice cream cone and a pair of jorts coming to all of them.

Katie's story illustrates how gratitude can leave an impression on the heart that lasts a lifetime, reminding us that small practices can make a big difference. In this next story, we hear how reciprocal learning applies to gratitude. Rachelle Dené Poth, teacher, author, speaker, and attorney, is a lifelong learner, and she shares how she continually learns from her high schoolers.

Getting Through by Expressing Gratitude

by Rachelle Dené Poth
Spanish and STEAM Teacher,
Attorney, Consultant
North Huntingdon, Pennsylvania

Sometimes life can be tough. We all go through challenges in our lives, whether personally or professionally. Professionally, challenges come in all forms with chaotic schedules, demands on our time, and days when getting it all done seems impossible. We all have days when we just don't feel like we can get through, and it can be overwhelming. It is important that we have strategies in place to push through whatever those challenges may be, and not just for our own well-being. Because of the role that we play in the lives of our students, we need to be at our best. Our students need us.

But how can we be at our best when we are experiencing challenges in our lives? It's the same for students. They enter our classrooms working through their own challenges, looking to us or their classmates for support. They learn from us, and the best thing we can do is listen, be present, and express gratitude. Expressing gratitude, something we can all practice and benefit from, helps us push through challenges.

A few years ago, I noticed my students expressing gratitude for the slightest things. I was inspired by the students who made a point each day to thank me for something. They thanked me for handing them papers, for teaching them, and in this school year, even for handing them paper towels to clean the desks. I would hear "thank you for today" as they left the classroom. At first, their thank-yous surprised me. I didn't expect it, and when they thanked me, I noticed how those two words made me feel. I felt valued and recognized for what I was trying to provide for them in class. I saw other students feel valued by their classmates. Because of my students, I became more intentional about expressing gratitude to others—to my family and friends, my students, and my colleagues. I noticed how it made me feel to show gratitude to others and the way that it made them feel. Even expressing gratitude to strangers who open a door or make space for you. Just saying thank you makes a difference.

When I think about challenging days, I realize that it was those moments and student interactions that made a difference. Those simple thank-yous from students helped to get me through. It does not take much, but it makes such an impact. Thanking students for even the littlest things, for something I noticed them doing in class to help others, for including their classmates, and sometimes just for making me laugh, matters. I show gratitude for students lightening class with humor, asking how I am doing, and for being a part of our class. I truly am thankful for what students have taught me and for lessons learned from them about the importance of showing gratitude.

These small thank-yous and acknowledgments make a difference. Hearing those words and saying them to another has a positive impact on the person receiving gratitude and on the person showing it. Each day I try to model showing gratitude and to think about the things in my life that I am thankful for.

I'm thankful for being an educator, for the students that I get to work with each day, and for the opportunity to make a difference. Taking small moments to show appreciation and to practice gratitude and kindness not only impacts those we interact with, but it elevates our mindset, pushing us through any challenge we may face and helping us embrace each day with a thankful heart and mind.

Rachelle's story is an inspiring example of learning about gratitude from and with kids. There is a lot we can learn from kids, and we also have the opportunity to empower our learners to teach others. One of the best examples of this empowerment I've seen comes from a collaboration between the Yale Center for Emotional Intelligence, Facebook, and Lady Gaga's Born This Way Foundation, which led to the creation of inspirED (ycei.org/inspired). inspirED provides free resources—designed by teens, educators, and SEL experts—to empower kids to work together to create a more positive school climate and foster greater well-being in their schools and communities.[1] inspirED is a beautiful example of cultivating a culture of emotional intelligence as well as learning from and with kids. What do you think your learners could teach you and your peers about gratitude and other social-emotional skills?

Teaching Kids to Be Grateful

As educators, we are also caregivers who play a huge role in developing the character of our learners. If you teach elementary, you probably spend five to six hours a day with kids Monday through Friday. If you teach secondary, you spend significant time with adolescents who are also in a crucial stage of development. Maybe you coach sports or lead after-school programs, which gives you even more time to make an impact. Plus, some kids have complicated situations at home, and you might be one of the most constant and positive adult figures in a child's life. Intentionally focusing on gratitude promotes social and emotional well-being in our learners and, if that isn't enough, it is also important for academics. We can nurture the whole child with gratitude!

According to Dr. Marc Brackett's research, emotions impact the following aspects of a child's development:

- Attention, memory, and learning
- Decision-making
- Relationship quality
- Physical and mental health
- Performance and creativity

If we are really focused on the whole child, we can't neglect our learners' emotions and well-being. We can nurture the whole child, tapping into the power of gratitude both as an emotion and a disposition.

IF WE ARE REALLY FOCUSED ON THE WHOLE CHILD, WE CAN'T NEGLECT OUR LEARNERS' EMOTIONS AND WELL-BEING. WE CAN NURTURE THE WHOLE CHILD, TAPPING INTO THE POWER OF GRATITUDE BOTH AS AN EMOTION AND A DISPOSITION.

Grateful to Learn

Thinking about gratitude for learning, I'm reminded of an old saying that I don't actually like, which is that education is wasted on the young. Education isn't transactional and it certainly isn't something that should be exclusive to certain populations. Education, and the sharing of ideas, is never wasted, but we know it can be much more productive when our learners are grateful for the opportunity to learn and are *awakened*, a concept presented by Dr. Kerry Howells. In her talk at TEDxLaunceston, "How Thanking Awakens Our Thinking," Dr. Howells shares three important things that she discovered:

- "The first one is that students by nature want to be awake, but they don't really know how to be. They want to be engaged, but they don't really know how to be and they're looking to us educators to teach them how.
- Secondly, teachers want to teach awake students, but they don't necessarily see that as part of their role nor do they know really how to bring that awake state to them.
- And the third thing is that, I believe in education, we've settled for far lower levels of awakeness in our students than what we should have."

Dr. Howells goes on to explain that in her quest to understand the relationship between gratitude and the awake state, she discovered that if we thank while we think, we think in a more awake and engaged way. After six years of studying gratitude and awakeness in education, Dr. Howells found that it is crucial that we focus on what happens before we start teaching. By preparing our innermost attitude for the activities to come, we have a richer, more engaging learning experience.[2] This seems simple enough, but is this happening in education?

My eight-year-old son, Blake, once asked me, "Mom, when do we use math in our lives?" Uh-oh, this sounds like a mom fail. Even if he hasn't seen these connections at school, his mom is a teacher. Yikes! For a bit of context, Blake is hardworking and loves math. He takes tremendous pride in his ability to tackle his math tasks easily, efficiently, and accurately. He is asking for the *why*, but this doesn't come from a place of "Why do I have to do this thing I don't like?" This is part of his inquisitive nature, and he is genuinely trying to make sense of where this content fits into his context. Naturally, when we are told to learn something and don't have an understanding of the purpose and value, it becomes difficult for learners of any age to fully appreciate it. We need to know our *why*.

Universal Design for Learning (UDL), which is based on neuroscience, is a research-based framework to optimize teaching and learning based on the three brain networks:

- Recognition (the *what* of learning)
- Strategic (the *how* of learning)
- Affective (the *why* of learning)

According to cast.org, "The goal of UDL is to support learners to become 'expert learners' who are, each in their own way, purposeful and motivated, resourceful and knowledgeable, and strategic and goal driven."[3] Practicing gratitude is directly connected to our affective networks, the part of the brain that manages interest, effort and persistence, and self-regulation. In other words, what we care about and our priorities. Learners are unique and dynamic in the ways they can be engaged or motivated to learn. We can offer multiple means of engagement and empower learners to bring their identities and interests into the learning. By planning activities with voice and choice, we strengthen relationships and develop expert learners who make connections between things they love and what we are learning. A simple example would be studying poetry and inviting learners to listen to their favorite songs, analyze the lyrics they find most interesting, and identify the rhyme schemes, or lack thereof.

By offering multiple means of engagement, learners can be grateful for the opportunity to learn and, to use Dr. Howells's words, they are awakened. Everything we are teaching should have a connection to the real world, so let's ignite the affective networks of the brain by starting with gratitude for the purpose and value of what we are learning.

A Thankful Learning Community

Gratitude for learning happens by preparing the internal attitude for what is coming in a lesson, but it can also be cultivated as we build and maintain a community of learners. We can use the Community of Inquiry (CoI) theoretical framework[4] to guide us in empowering learners, nurturing the whole child, and fostering thankfulness.

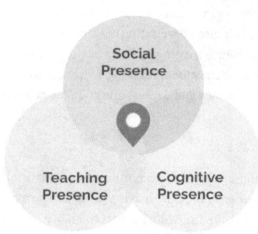

Here is CoI defined in the context of gratitude:

Teaching Presence

- Building and maintaining a one-to-one relationship with each learner, we can establish respect and rapport, which leads to mutual appreciation.
- Developing a communication and feedback process that ensures frequent, high-quality interactions with each student, learners can feel seen, heard, known, and valued.

- Demonstrating unconditional positive regard, we can show complete support, acceptance, and appreciation for each individual.

Social Presence

- Providing time and space for peers to collaborate, we can develop a sense of belonging while also embracing and protecting individual identities and contributions. Note: Practicing gratitude does not mean we have to be self-effacing. We can be grateful to others for their contributions while also appreciating what we bring to the community.
- Establishing a trusting learning environment through embedded social-emotional learning (e.g., signature practices), we can experience and express gratitude for each other.

Cognitive Presence

- Collaborating and communicating, we can coconstruct knowledge and skills to achieve our academic goals. We can celebrate our individual achievements as well as our collective achievements.

Gratitude at Every Age and Stage

Gratitude is not only the greatest of the virtues, but the parent of all of the others.

—Cicero (106–43BC)

When it comes to learning with gratitude, there are ways we can support kids at different ages and stages while also empowering them. We need to:

- promote self-efficacy and collective efficacy
- have high expectations, remove barriers, and be aware of developmental appropriateness in order to strategically insert ourselves
- allow for productive struggle to nurture independence
- use a systemic SEL approach to develop positive characteristics

The study of gratitude in kids is still relatively new, but research by Jeffrey J. Froh, PsyD, and Giacomo Bono, PhD, finds that the benefits of cultivating gratitude in students are significant. Here are considerations for the developmental stages of gratitude:

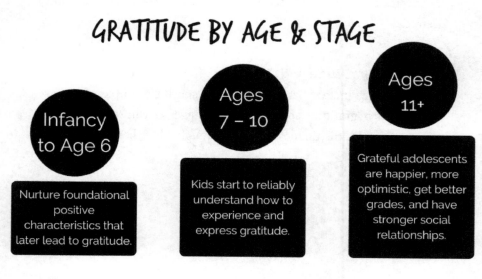

GRATITUDE BY AGE & STAGE

Infancy to Age 6
Nurture foundational positive characteristics that later lead to gratitude.

Ages 7 – 10
Kids start to reliably understand how to experience and express gratitude.

Ages 11+
Grateful adolescents are happier, more optimistic, get better grades, and have stronger social relationships.

- Infancy to age six: Nurture the development of foundational positive characteristics that later lead to deep and authentic gratitude.
- Ages seven to ten: Kids start to reliably understand how to experience and express gratitude.

- Ages eleven and older: Those who have developed a grateful disposition are happier, more optimistic, and get better grades compared to their peers who are less grateful. They also have stronger social relationships.[5]

Gratitude research points to the importance of theory of mind, the ability to understand that individuals (including ourselves) have unique beliefs, intents, desires, emotions, and knowledge. According to Froh and Bono, theory of mind is present in children by about age five, and it is a critical precursor to gratitude because it allows children to appreciate the positive intentions and motivations of others. Knowing this, we can embed SEL practices that promote social awareness, such as empathy and perspective-taking, as we nurture the whole child. Visit casel.org and search for the "SEL 3 Signature Practices Playbook" for specific practices that you can bring into your learning community every day.

Stories of Gratitude with Kids

The educator vignettes that follow provide specific examples and share the nuances of gratitude at every age and stage. As you read, I encourage you to notice the themes that run through all of them.

Growing Gratitude from the Start in Preschool

by Naomi Toland

Head Teacher
Auckland, New Zealand

A few years ago, we set up a gratitude garden in our learning space with the goal of weaving empathy into our lessons to foster the learners' inner and outer voices.

Every learner has their own section within the garden, and each week we wrote notes expressing something we were grateful for.

When dealing with emotional regulation and feelings, I sometimes speak about needing to dial up and dial down the experiences. Occasionally learners must dial up the amount of emotional regulation they need; for example, if they are going through a challenging time, they may need to dial up their capacity to seek perspectives or have gratitude. But in other moments, they may need to dial down their need for emotional regulation because they are in a safe and wholesome place, so they can just get on with their day-to-day lives.

In the beginning, we were doing our gratitude garden every day, and this was good because the learners had intensive opportunities to immerse themselves and explore what gratitude is. But eventually we realized that doing it every day had made the task become less meaningful because the learners were running out of ideas. As a result, we started doing it weekly. When it was time, we reflected on the days gone by and noted down what we were grateful for.

We also began by giving the learners examples of what they could be grateful for, gifting them vocabulary, until eventually they started to see and speak about their own experiences more naturally.

In the display we had various items:

- Mirrors so learners could look at themselves and catch their negative self-talk and reflect on their thinking
- Quotes that the learners could add to, to give themselves and their peers inspiration
- A gratitude book where the learners could share what they were grateful for and, in times of need or just if they wanted, they could go back and remind themselves what they were grateful for.

The teachers also had their own avatars, so we could all come together and learn with one another, making this a great individual and shared experience.

A Jar Full of Change for an Elementary Schoolhouse

by Sean Gaillard

Elementary Principal, Author, and Podcaster
Clemmons, North Carolina

"Mr. Gaillard, did you read my gratitude slip?"

This question is now symphonic to my ears. I greet it not only with gratitude for the grace that resonates within it but also with hope. With the residue of COVID-19 still impacting the collective psyche of educators everywhere, gratitude has been far from the lexicon of schoolhouses. Despite that painful reality, a slip of paper dropped in a mason jar has transformed our school culture.

As principal, I look for entry points to ignite change and synergy in ways that keep our students at the center of our schoolhouse. In this age of anxiety for our teachers, I know that small moments of inspiration matter. I do my best to add something to their professional dashboard beyond what I place in my weekly memo blog. I provide a section in that blog entitled "For Your Toolbox." One day, I added an inspiring Edutopia article on how adding gratitude to the mix of a school culture can be transformative.[6] I didn't expect any fanfare for the article, but something extraordinary happened.

Our art teacher stopped me to share something she had created. It was a mason jar painted with a few color designs. On it was painted the word *Gratitude*. Inside the jar were various slips of paper. The art teacher shared that she was inspired by the article she read embedded in the weekly memo blog. She wanted to add to our school culture efforts by adding gratitude to the mix. Her idea was to have students write down something they were grateful for as they entered the classroom and then place their gratitude slips in the jar. The art teacher asked if I would randomly draw slips and read the grateful words of our students during morning announcements.

I was moved by this and readily agreed.

What followed was a simple act that became a beacon of hope for our students. As I read over the hundreds of gratitude slips our students had written, I was captivated by the personal things they were sharing. Students were expressing gratitude for friends, family, even their pets. I was honored to read them over the loudspeaker and privileged to share such personal expressions of gratitude on behalf of our students. I felt like I was doing something important, almost sacred. Here, I was giving voice to the words of our students as they were expressing their sincere appreciation for those that had a profound impact on their lives.

As the days progressed, I noticed that more students were coming up to me and asking me if I would read their gratitude slip. Dozens of students approached me with pride over their gratitude statement. It was an entry point for me to build kinship with the students I served.

As a quick aside, I do the morning announcements from various classrooms; our loudspeaker system permits me to do that. Reading those gratitude slips over the loudspeaker in front of students makes the experience of gratitude even more significant. I see the anticipation on student faces, and I can feel a visceral vibe in the air.

Reading gratitude slips may not seem like an earth-shattering practice. There are no technical bells or whistles. But it is all rooted in simplicity. Gratitude is a portal to empathy for others. Students sharing and learning about what others are grateful for stirs connection. Teachers have another entryway to build connections by hearing the sincere and loving words our students are writing. Gratitude does build character for our students, but it also creates an awareness of others. Seeing the good that someone else has added to one's life is a valuable lesson not only for students, but also for teachers.

Building school culture does not have to be an event rooted in confetti and selfies posted on social media. Rather, it is putting values into sincere, dynamic action. Adding gratitude to the mix of our school culture has proven to be a game changer for the schoolhouse I serve. Sharing gratitude has created more connectedness to the school culture we are building together.

One idea from a teacher sparked inspiration for our entire school. For that move, I am eternally grateful. I think of the ripple effect that resonates from our art teacher to the students, encouraging them to practice gratitude for a lifetime.

Seeing Through the Smokescreens in Middle School

by Chey Cheney and
Pawan (Pav) Wander

Middle School Teachers, Authors, and Podcasters
Toronto, Ontario, Canada

Acts of gratitude can seem so simple that they can become trivial. Because of this, gratitude can sometimes be one of the first tools on our teacher tool belts to be dropped in practice. The impact of gratefulness, the ability for it to foster deep and meaningful relationships, and its power to change the course of an individual's day can be forgotten when other areas of concern dominate the learning space. We have come to realize that the act of gratitude, when performed with sincerity and purpose, and the equally important act of learning how to receive it with pure appreciation, is foundational to quality teaching and for cementing powerful learning environments.

As adults, we have a tendency to forget that students are on the journey of self-actualization, and there is perhaps no age of students that is more explorative or has a more heightened awareness of their self-actualization than middle school students. Constantly affirming and reaffirming their identities, kids between the ages of eleven and fourteen spend much of their existence attempting to articulate who they are and what it is they strive to achieve.

Middle school and young adolescence is an anxiety-ridden and stressful time, and students always assume that everything they do is being watched and judged. That reality, coupled with the awkwardness that can surround giving and receiving thanks and complimentary words, highlights the difficulties with embedding gratitude in a middle school culture and building up students' self-confidence to express thankfulness with sincerity.

As teachers in the middle school space, you always need to be mindful that underlying social pressure to appear a certain way can make it particularly difficult for students to display acts of gratitude. It's imperative for teachers to intentionally create a culture of gratitude in the learning space. We need to be able to explain it, model it, and use it with frequency, both formally and informally, and most certainly to honor it when it is given back to us.

One powerful way we have embedded gratitude in our teaching is to take full advantage of informal transition times. We use this time to be purposeful in reaching out and connecting with students. Perhaps we use this time to share moments of gratitude for completed schoolwork or for their efforts. We might even embrace a salutation or question while validating and affirming the great work they've been doing in class.

For example, we often take advantage of the transition time first thing in the morning, when students are lined up at the morning bell. We go out and we greet them, using this time to connect with each student and affirm gratitude before even entering the school. We are able to make those first interactions with the middle school students authentically positive. We recall so vividly when we began this activity that students were often speechless, unsure of how to respond and apprehensive to show any emotion or appreciation in return. This often manifested as a mumbled thank-you as they scurried ahead.

It's crucial for teachers to maintain this practice of gratitude and not be dissuaded by an initial lack of interaction from students. The reciprocity will indeed manifest and be actualized, but it is important to be mindful of how acts of gratitude land on middle school students. As you make repeated efforts to share validating statements about the quality of their work and comment on their positive character traits, the apprehension that lies within an adolescent learner will begin to dissipate. They'll soon be more open to receiving. The safety they feel will begin to permeate, and eventually the students will learn to give back and show reciprocity.

Gratitude is foundational with middle school learners. The barriers and obstacles they often put up before allowing themselves to receive and give gratitude are simply smokescreens. They are going through a vast amount of personal growth and discovery and are more concerned with and aware of their surroundings than at any other age. If we can commit ourselves to the relentless pursuit of gratitude as a culture in our learning spaces, it will benefit both teachers and students. We may not see those dividends right away, but they will be appreciated and reciprocated if we stay true to the foundational concept and practice of gratitude.

Being Grateful for the Wins and the Fails in High School

by Stacey Roshan

High School Director of Innovation and EdTech
Boyds, Maryland

When we give kids the right platforms to share in a format that is comfortable to them, they can open up and learn to express themselves in whole new ways. This is critical in helping students self-reflect, regulate their emotions, and build relational skills (all fundamentals of SEL).

A powerful moment for me was when I started having students record mini video check-ins as part of our class routine. I kept the prompt open-ended enough to let students freely share what was on their minds but also framed the prompt to help students get started. I've learned how important it is to properly frame a prompt to strike that delicate balance—leave things too open and students can feel paralyzed to start, make things too tight and your rubric becomes a checklist that students follow.

I started by having students share their wins and fails from the week. Sometimes, I asked students to make this response specific to the course, and other times I asked students to simply reflect on their week. I would switch things up between a written response and video response and, later in the year, allowed them to choose their preferred format. Giving students a variety of ways to express themselves and forcing them to try various approaches is important as they self-discover what feels best to them.

Talk about a Failure
- What's a major fail you had this week?
- How did your initial approach to the problem or situation lead you astray?
- How has your approach to the problem or situation changed now? How has your thinking shifted?
- What is one thing you can take away as a lesson learned from this fail? How can you turn this into a future win?

Talk about a Win
- What's a major win you had this week?
- How did your initial approach to the problem or situation lead to your success?
- What is one thing you can take away as a lesson learned from this win? How can you apply this lesson to help you find future successes?

This activity gives me insight into what students are dealing with beyond what I see in the classroom and helps me develop a more holistic, trusting relationship with my students. Importantly, their reflections tie into a practice of gratitude and reflection. And though I never framed this as a gratitude activity in my classroom, at its core, this activity encouraged students to think about what they were grateful for in their week. As students talked through their major wins, most of the time they talked about doing good for others. After all, doing something for another person is a powerful boost to our physical and mental well-being and one of the first things that comes to mind when we think about a highlight from our week.

Seeing the power of this activity in my classroom gave me an idea to extend this further and to use it with my own young nieces who live on the opposite coast. Could some of the lessons I learned from my high school students apply to preschool and elementary-age kids, too? The answer is a resounding yes.

When I started incorporating video check-ins in my classes, I suddenly heard students share in a way I had never experienced before. Some of the quietest students in class would share the most detailed replies on video. So when I was having trouble getting my nieces to open up over the phone or on Zoom, I turned to video in the same way. I started with a gratitude prompt that I asked the whole family to respond to. From there, we did a kindness challenge. And then, everyone recorded a simple share-out of a highlight from our day.

It was remarkable to see my nieces open up on the videos they recorded. If you were to catch them on a Zoom call, you'd think they are camera shy. But put them in front of the video camera, where they are the center of attention, and allow them to hit the record button, and things quickly change! Not only is all attention on them, but they can also apply filters and other fun effects to their recording. The kicker is that they can watch themselves (on loop)! What's powerful about this, particularly when guided, is that we can have important conversations to help them further self-reflect and gain better self-awareness as they watch their playback.

Notice how these stories illustrate the developmental journey that starts with character building and modeling in the younger grades and moves into deeper self-discovery in middle school and high school. In all of these examples we see that gratitude can:

- be both an individual and shared experience
- nurture relationships
- shift a classroom or school culture with small practices
- create a learning environment where all feel seen, heard, known, and valued

Regardless of the age and stage, we can practice gratitude to establish psychological safety, nurture a sense of belonging, and activate learning.

Even More Gratitude Practices with Kids

These educators shared specific gratitude practices that have worked with their learners. There are many more ways that we can practice gratitude for and with kids. Here are a couple of my favorites before we shift to discussing gratitude with peers.

- **Positive Calls or Messages Home** (Gratitude for Kids) If you are a parent of school-age children, you know that feeling when you see their school's phone number appear on your phone. Immediately your amygdala starts to alert your nervous system, and the fear kicks in. Personally, I have a physical reaction that I feel ripple through my body. Are they hurt or sick? Did they do something wrong? But imagine if that call were a positive call. We can call home to express gratitude for so many things—for that extra effort shown, for being kind and helpful to peers, for consistently contributing to class conversations. This small, sincere act of gratitude takes a little bit of time, but it can completely shift the dynamic in the home-school connection.

- **Word Clouds** (Gratitude with Kids) I'm obsessed with word clouds! The ability to ask an open-ended question and create a visual representation of the answers, where the more often a specific word is used, the larger it appears, is magical to me. I've used this with kids and adults to create a gratitude gift for students, teachers, principals, custodians, paraprofessionals, parent volunteers, guest speakers, and pretty much anyone who is part of our learning community. Here is an example of a prompt I typically use: write the first few (nice) words that come to mind for our hard-working custodian.

If my group needs a little help, we brainstorm together, or I give them a list of positive personality adjectives to pull from. These word clouds are always so special that I like to print them and frame them!

CHAPTER 4

Gratitude with Peers

> *Feeling gratitude and not expressing it is like wrapping a present and not giving it.*
> —William Arthur Ward

Profound Gratitude

Like family, those we work with on a regular basis can be the ones we express gratitude to the least. It is not necessarily for lack of feeling gratitude. It can actually come from having such profound gratitude that you don't even know how to express it.

Early in my career, I had the incredible opportunity to teach at a brand new school. Even more amazingly, my friend Colleen Kelly Gurney was also hired to teach the same grade. Since our new campus was still under construction when the school year started, we were temporarily housed on another campus. Space was limited, so Colleen and I shared an old middle school science classroom. Yes, we had two full classes combined into one room, but it was a large classroom and we made it work. More than that, we took full advantage of the situation.

Officially, we were rostered separate sets of second graders, but Colleen and I leveraged this unique opportunity to coteach rather than just share space. We got very creative with planning projects, small group instruction, and one-on-one support. (There is a lot you can do with two teachers in the same room!) I truly believe we did great things for our learners, but it's very possible that I learned more than anyone during this time. Not only did Colleen and I collaborate on everything, but I also got a front-row seat to watch a gifted teacher in action on a daily basis. Without question, it was the best professional learning experience of my life.

With gratitude that profound, it's overwhelming and difficult to find the right words and the right way to share the feelings. I know I didn't show Colleen enough gratitude when we were teaching together, so I'll take the opportunity right here, right now to express my gratitude. As a person and an educator Colleen's positive attitude, enthusiasm, and kindness radiate. It is infectious! I witnessed her work tirelessly and creatively to make sure that our learners were always getting the best education possible and, as a coteacher, she was a generous collaborator who was patient with me every single day. I have tinkered with this paragraph many times, and it still doesn't feel like enough. I don't think anything I write could ever be enough, but I hope she reads this and understands how much I cherish her as a colleague and a lifelong friend.

Do We Have to Be Grateful for Everyone?

I have been blessed to work with Colleen and many other exceptional educators. But not everyone we work with is destined to be our lifelong friend. Perhaps you actually dislike a team member. Maybe this person drives you crazy, and you can't imagine being grateful for them. Guess what? It's time to return to VIA's character strengths from the previous chapter and, just like we did for the kids who challenge us, look for the positives in our peers. I'm not suggesting that you become besties with everyone, but it really is true that the best way to change someone else's behavior is to change our own behavior first. Plus, we never really know what is going on with others, and maybe this person is going through personal or professional adversity that you don't know about. A little bit of genuine gratitude from an unexpected source could possibly help.

> **Nothing more detestable does the earth produce than an ungrateful man.**
>
> **—Decimius Magnus Ausonius**

Now, if you are struggling with someone who you pour a lot into, but this person never reciprocates or shows appreciation, you have my total empathy. I like to think that I'm not a terribly judgmental person, but I'm a guardian of justice to a fault when it comes to gratitude. This gives me little to no tolerance for ingratitude and people who feel entitled. Often the end result is suffering for me and total unawareness for the other person. When this happens, I'm letting them rent space in my head for free. My best advice is to stop waiting for signs of appreciation. That doesn't mean we stop working with them (we may not have a choice), and it doesn't mean we stop treating them well, but it does mean we need to adjust our expectations. We are here to serve kids and our learning community. We do what we do for the good of our stakeholders, not for recognition, right?

> **Act with kindness, but do not expect gratitude.**
>
> **—Confucius**

In my experience, those who are completely ungrateful and feel truly entitled are few and far between. (Thankfully!) Most who do not express gratitude simply do not have gratitude as a habit or a disposition. The good news is that gratitude is contagious! We can make it a point to practice gratitude with our peers in one-on-one situations, in team meetings, and as a staff. We can also make being thankful part of our culture by creating rituals and routines. For example, gratitude practices can be intentionally and explicitly integrated throughout staff meetings and professional learning in meaningful ways. As I shared in chapter 2, I use CASEL's three SEL signature practices whenever I work with kids or adults, so consider making gratitude practices part of your welcoming inclusion activity, engaging strategies, or optimistic closure when you gather.

THE BEST WAY TO CHANGE SOMEONE ELSE'S BEHAVIOR IS TO CHANGE OUR OWN BEHAVIOR FIRST

Dr. Christine Olmstead, associate superintendent of educational services at Orange County Department of Education, shared with me that her team is very intentional in creating space for gratitude. They regularly dedicate ten minutes at the beginning of their meetings for leaders to pause and express thanks. How gratitude is expressed is up to each individual. They can write thank-you cards, send text messages or emails of appreciation, or use their "awesomeness notebooks" to plan for how they will show gratitude in the upcoming week. This could happen in schools with principals giving teachers time at the beginning of staff meetings to express gratitude to kids and peers. This simple practice can have a huge impact on culture.

From Surviving to Thriving and Flourishing

At times our own light goes out and is rekindled by a spark from another person. Each of us has cause to think with deep gratitude of those who have lighted flame within us.

—Albert Schweitzer

Gratitude for peers isn't just a *nice to have*. Members of our profession are truly struggling right now. Educators are suffering from disengagement due to burnout, compassion fatigue, and even first-hand trauma. According to educator and author Mandy Froehlich, "Educator disengagement is an emotional detachment from teaching. Usually, this detachment happens without realizing we're doing it in order to protect ourselves from further hurt."

A RAND survey conducted in early 2021 found that nearly one in four teachers said that they were likely to leave their jobs by the end of the 2020–21 school year.[1] Even before the COVID-19 global pandemic, the average was still one in six. We lose teachers for a variety of reasons, and some stay even though they are unhappy out of the necessity for income. However, practicing gratitude can mitigate a number of these issues by helping us to cope with stress, regulate our emotions, nurture relationships, and reengage us as educators, which all lead to increased resilience and improved well-being. The Greater Good Science Center's gratitude curricula, available at ggsc.berkeley .edu, explains that research proves teachers who practice gratitude "feel more satisfied and accomplished, and less emotionally exhausted, possibly reducing teacher burnout."[2] We can use gratitude to help us shift from barely surviving to actually thriving and flourishing, getting back to the joy of teaching, learning, and leading.

Stories of Gratitude with Peers

The educator stories that follow are examples of how uniquely each individual and school can approach gratitude with peers. (I did promise that we would keep that theme of *equifinality* shared in chapter 1, right?) And while the strategies for fostering gratitude are different in these vignettes, the intentions are authentic and altruistic, which lead to a thankful community.

Small Gestures for a Culture of Caring and a Sense of Belonging

by Dwight Carter

Director of Student Support Systems and Author
Blacklick, Ohio

There is so much power in a handwritten note. A handwritten note takes time, intentionality, and care. When I was a principal, I showed my appreciation for my staff by writing them notes of gratitude and attaching a small gold lapel star to the envelope.

I ordered some cards and matching envelopes with our school logo from a local company and a large bag of gold stars online. I stored both items in one of my desk drawers for safekeeping and easy access. I didn't have a scheduled day of the week to write the notes. I noticed that when I felt overwhelmed or somewhat down, I'd go to the drawer, pull out a few cards, and reflect. I would think about what I had observed as I visited classrooms and attended cocurricular or extracurricular events, and I thought about the conversations I had had with various staff members. I'd jot down a few things on a Post-it to capture my thoughts. Then, I'd start writing thank-you cards to the people that came to mind: a teacher who facilitated an engaging lesson, a secretary who provided impeccable service, a cafeteria staff member who enthusiastically greeted students, a custodian who went above and beyond to meet the needs of others, or an assistant principal who handled a difficult situation with patience and poise.

Once I sealed the envelope, I'd pin a gold star to it and then walk to deliver the cards to each individual. While I didn't stay to see them open and read it, I know they appreciated it because I'd see the gold star pinned to their lanyard or name badge, and later I'd see the card displayed on their desk or work area. (It is important to note that you want to ensure you authentically acknowledge everyone over time.)

There are a couple of benefits to this practice. First, I immediately felt better and reenergized when I took the time to write the notes. I had a more positive outlook, felt more confident, and was happier overall. Second, the people who received the messages knew I genuinely appreciated them and their contributions to our school culture. I know because they would eventually stop by my office, or we'd chat when we saw each other around the school, and they would thank me for the note. It was a small gesture that made a huge impact.

A simple act of appreciation goes a long way in creating a culture of caring and a sense of belonging. When staff and faculty are appreciated, they feel seen, heard, valued, and respected, which leads to a more significant contribution. The more they contribute to the school, the better the culture is for students. I noticed that teachers took more risks by trying new strategies, proposing new classes, or being open to different ideas. Our custodians took more pride in creating a clean and welcoming environment, our assistant principals would take on a little more and stay a little longer with a challenging situation, and generally, more people would show appreciation for others. The more the adults feel cared for, the better the culture is for student learning.

Tell Me Something Good

by Katie Martin

Educator, Author, and Chief Impact Officer
San Diego, California

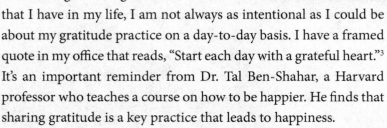

Even though I am grateful for so much that I have in my life, I am not always as intentional as I could be about my gratitude practice on a day-to-day basis. I have a framed quote in my office that reads, "Start each day with a grateful heart."[3] It's an important reminder from Dr. Tal Ben-Shahar, a Harvard professor who teaches a course on how to be happier. He finds that sharing gratitude is a key practice that leads to happiness.

Gratitude, I think, is simple and complex at the same time. It's simple in that we just need to acknowledge something that someone else has done. Yet, this simple act requires vulnerability to go beyond feeling grateful to actually express that gratitude. To acknowledge someone else's impact on you means that you received help or guidance or something from someone else. We often have defense mechanisms in place to shield us from vulnerability, but choosing instead to lean into it is exactly what allows us to create more connection, joy, and happiness.

This was reinforced for me when I had a colleague go out of his way to help me with some back-end issues I was having with my blog and emails. Asking for help was hard to begin with, but I could not figure this out on my own, and he was able to figure it out quickly. I was so grateful for his expertise and willingness to troubleshoot for me. Without too much thought, I sent an email to thank him for his support. A few days later he called and shared that he was really struggling and my email had made his day. I was kind of shocked because all I had done was say thanks, but he reminded me of a time that I had gone out of my way to help him that I had not remembered. It was a reminder that you never know the impact you might have on someone, and sharing gratitude can have ripple effects that you may never truly comprehend.

This experience pushed me to be more intentional in my work with administrators, teachers, and students and to create more opportunities to share gratitude and celebrate our successes. As we evolve in education, it's important to not just focus on what needs to change or the multitude of struggles that exist. I often start conversations by saying, "Tell me something good," which is something I say to my own kids regularly. We are conditioned to focus on what is *not* working and to pinpoint all the things that have gone wrong, as opposed to what is going well or even the simple steps we have taken in the right direction. So often, people freeze when they are asked to highlight the things that are going well, or they just revert back to a challenge. But knowing the benefits this gratitude mindset has on our well-being and happiness, I push each person to focus on some success, growth, or positive moment. As the momentum shifts, people start to smile and engage differently. Focusing on gratitude and what is working doesn't mean that we ignore challenges, it just means we choose to build on a foundation of what we have, successes we have experienced, and the strengths of individuals and their contributions.

When we focus on the good and celebrate it, we can change a person's outlook, cultivate relationships, and spread more love in our schools and communities. There are many reasons to be grateful if we are open to them. We can use joyful moments to feed our souls and lift up others. This is a reminder to myself as much as it is to you that we need to constantly embrace vulnerability; by not just feeling grateful but by actually expressing our gratitude, we create more happiness in our lives and the lives of others.

Dance Parties and Giving Recognition

by Lauren Kaufman

Assistant Principal and Writer
Lido Beach, New York

The trajectory of my career has guided me to pathways of meaningful, magical moments. These moments opened doors to self-discovery, deep reflection, and encounters with people who have illuminated what it means to show and feel gratitude. The genuine experiences and interactions I've encountered throughout my educational journey have offered a beautiful opportunity to pay it forward and lean in to make a positive impact on the greatest gifts: learners, colleagues, communities, and the organizations I've proudly served. I always remember the people who have supported my continual growth and development. Without the nurturing encouragement of mentors and colleagues who have graciously and empathetically shown me the way, it may have been difficult to persevere through the challenges educators can endure.

When I unwrap these vivid moments of gratitude in my mind, I can still feel the immense joy of what it meant to be gifted with recognition and appreciation for my efforts. In my earliest years of teaching, I savored these moments of gratitude as they developed my confidence and cemented a strong foundation, allowing me to profoundly reflect on the educator I was and wanted to be. Do you think about the people who have made an impact on your professional journey? These are moments you bottle up and relive in your memory because they meant so much. When you need inspiration, reach for those moments.

My collection of memorable moments of gratitude helped me frame the work I did in the mentor program I facilitated. I chose to emphasize the value of the teacher induction process and preparing new teachers to have long, meaningful careers. I did not take this job lightly. Not. One. Bit. I had an undeniable vision to create engaging learning experiences that fostered a community of support, while giving new and veteran teachers a toolbox of strategies they could implement and embed into their daily practices. It was my mission to create a safe environment by warmly welcoming all mentors and mentees into inclusive physical and virtual spaces. What is one way I did this? Music and dancing! To me, what is life without music? Can you visualize entering a physical or virtual space during a mentor meeting and seeing me dancing and lip-synching to a fun song while greeting everyone by name? I learned that this act of silliness influenced many teachers to rush to a meeting in anticipation of what song would be played and how I'd interact with them. This small act of gratitude rallied people together, put smiles on teachers' faces, sparked innovative spirits, and became a powerful investment in the emotional deposit box! Many teachers even shared that they employed this practice of gratitude with students to build connections that also gave them time for movement over the course of the day.

Another important act of gratitude . . . give recognition! It is human nature to want to feel valued and acknowledged. I always highlight teacher leaders' small and big wins. And yes, if you work with kids, consider yourself a leader! Everyone within an educational organization works tirelessly to meet the needs of their learners. For that, they deserve to be celebrated every chance you get! At mentor meetings, I'd highlight the work they had been employing in their classrooms by looking through the mentor program hashtag #LBLeads and Twitter handle @LBMentorProgram I created, taking screenshots of their tweets and placing them on a few slides with GIFs of fireworks. This was an opportunity to encourage various teachers to spotlight instructional practices with their colleagues. For the educators who were not on social media, I'd have them send me pictures of their work and their permission to share it. The impact of this practice was monumental, and the cross-pollination of ideas within our own professional learning communities and beyond was inspiring. I even saw high school teachers trying practices that elementary teachers were implementing. What are some ways you can publicly recognize the incredible work educators implement in their classrooms?

Teaching is not just something you do; it's a calling; it's a beautiful gift. It's an opportunity to build social capital and unlock human potential. Be the person who makes others smile when they need it most. Be the person who elevates your colleagues and celebrates their accomplishments. Be the educator you always needed. *You* have the ability to create pathways of meaningful magical moments that can leave everlasting legacies in the hearts and minds of everyone you serve!

Gratitude Is Contagious

by Bobby Pollicino
Head of Upper School
Poolesville, Maryland

In the fall of 2016, I was in my seventeenth year as an educator and my second year as a division director. But I really hadn't thought much about how I got there, why I was there, or where gratitude fit into everything. It took a seemingly innocuous question for me to come to this realization.

During an administrative team meeting, the head of school asked, "Bobby, do you have your finger on the pulse of your faculty?" I replied, "No." People were surprised at my candor and puzzled at my response. I continued, "It's not because I do not think about it or don't care, and it's not because I don't want them to be heard or be successful." In truth, it just wasn't how I was raised.

I grew up in a blue-collar middle-class family as the son of a US marine and combat veteran of Vietnam. It was a time when feelings were not as important as getting the job done. That mindset allowed me to have a successful high school and college career as a student athlete. It also led me to various leadership roles in education. It was my expectation that everyone would come to school and do their jobs, regardless of how they felt. I transitioned from dean of students and head varsity lacrosse coach to a new leadership role without considering how it impacted my responsibilities. As you would expect, it was a rough transition that first year, and it would be an understatement to say my emotional intelligence was not fully developed!

I was very fortunate to participate in a professional learning opportunity the next summer where I could detach and realize why I needed to do more *maintenance* work with the faculty. It can't be task-focused work all the time. The focus has to go beyond entering grades, writing lessons, getting to meetings on time, etc. The maintenance piece, the emotional piece, the social-emotional learning with the faculty had been missing.

As I reflected on my experience that summer, I realized that I needed to make some changes to benefit our faculty and also my own personal life. So, I started a gratitude journal. If you had asked me about gratitude journals five years ago, I would have told you it was pointless, and I didn't have time for it. I definitely wouldn't have believed it could have an impact on my life or those around me. That summer I started journaling every day. It's now part of my morning routine before anyone else wakes up. At the end of my journal entry, I answer this question: What are three things you're grateful for today? I can count on one hand how many times I have missed a day since 2017. It completely changed my mindset, and I began recognizing what people around me were doing, what they were feeling, and how they were impacted by the environment around them. I realized that I needed to do more. I needed to help people understand how reflection and expressing gratitude can help others. These behaviors and actions are so important as a leader, and I was failing to do them. In reflecting on why I was failing, I realized it came from past experiences and my bias about what was needed to be successful as a leader and team builder. I needed to make some changes.

To that end, I started adding shout-outs in my weekly emails to the faculty. Folio, the program we use to document goals and professional development, includes a spotlight feature where anybody can send a compliment to a colleague—which also goes to their supervisor.

The adult conversation around gratitude now impacts student conversations. Our National Honor Society (NHS) started a new tradition in 2021. NHS students placed boxes and sheets of paper around campus, and they asked peers to write a gratitude note about someone in the community. Every Friday at assembly, four NHS members get up on stage and each read a gratitude note. It has been amazing to see the smiles on peoples' faces and the cheers from the audience. Our students now recognize the importance of gratitude and sharing it with others.

Gratitude is contagious and impacts every aspect of our school community. When you appreciate what you have, you do not focus on what you lack. It has allowed us to continue to grow and develop even in the most difficult times.

As we saw with the stories of gratitude with kids shared in chapter 3, the practices vary, but the focus is on making sure everyone feels seen, heard, known, and valued. The simple yet profound acts of gratitude that these educators do for their peers have untold ripple effects. The positivity shared impacts those directly involved, and it also spreads throughout the learning community and beyond.

Parents and Families as Peers

When we talk about gratitude with peers, I want to point out that not all of our peers attend the faculty meeting. Parents and families are the first-and-forever teachers of our learners, and they can often be underutilized and underappreciated. One way to show gratitude to our families is by making sure they also feel seen, heard, known, and valued. Just as our kids need to be noticed and appreciated, so do their families. And there is so much we can learn from our students' families when we partner with them in developing the whole child.

Paige Couros is an educator sharing her perspective as a parent cultivating gratitude with her young children. She is exceptional in both roles, and this is just one example of how we can learn from the families of our students.

Giggles Leading to Gratitude

by Paige Couros

Teacher, Mother, and Publisher
Edmonton, Alberta, Canada

Do you ever feel like you do too much for your kids? You cook and clean and entertain them, all while maintaining a household and their extracurriculars? Some days, does it feel like it's so defeating that you want to just lie on the floor and let them fend for themselves? No, just me? Okay, I'll get off the floor!

A few months ago, I felt like I just completely lost my connection to my daughter. I had just had another baby, and she was getting older and didn't need me as much. I felt like I spent any time I had, that I wasn't with the baby, trying to do fun things for my older daughter. The problem was, I wasn't modeling gratitude or teaching her how to be grateful, so she just wasn't. It hurt my feelings, and she was always wanting more, never satisfied with all the things that I was doing for her. I tried getting her to state what she was grateful for, but in all honesty, that wasn't very effective because I hadn't taught her how to notice things she was grateful for, nor did I teach her how to show her gratitude.

What is the old adage? Do what I say, not what I do. Unfortunately, that never works with children, so we truly have to model for them what gratitude looks like. There are few things in this world that my girls love more than when I am silly. I know that when I model gratitude, the more I ham it up and the more I make it silly, the more memorable it is for them. Don't get me wrong, I am not inauthentic when I do it, I just make sure that it is really clear and memorable.

Yesterday, I let my daughter make my coffee (teach them early, am I right?), and when she handed it to me and I took a sip, I closed my eyes and said, "I love you, coffee . . . coffee, you make me so happy, and I just can't live without you. DON'T EVER LEAVE ME, COFFEE!" Both of my girls thought this was hilarious and were giggling like crazy. (If there were such a thing as a comedian for under-five-year-olds, I would be on tour, but sadly there just isn't a market for it.) A few hours later, my daughter Kallea was helping me set up our Christmas houses and she said, "Oh, Christmas houses, you bring me such joy! I wish you could stay with us all year," and then I said, "DON'T EVER LEAVE, CHRISTMAS HOUSES!"

By showing my gratitude (in a somewhat over-the-top manner), it was memorable to my daughter and a fun way for her to express her gratitude. She was able to share her gratitude and joy for what we were doing because she had a way that she felt comfortable using. That night, when I asked her what she was grateful for that day, without a second thought, she said, "Setting up the Christmas houses with you." She was able to remember what she was grateful for because we made the act of showing gratitude so memorable. I do the same thing with many other simple things in our lives. When the sun sets, I always call the girls over to watch it with me and I say, "Isn't this the best? I am so happy to get to watch the sunset with you!"

When we model gratitude for our kids and make it accessible to them, it makes it easier for them to show their gratitude as well! Give it a try!

I love how Paige reminds us that our kids are, well, kids! We should never forget about the importance of play and laughter for all ages and stages. There's also a lesson of tailoring to individual needs. What works for one kid may not work for another, so finding a variety of ways to model gratitude is important.

As we invite families to be partners in gratitude, we can also learn about and honor the diversity in cultural practices of gratitude. There are typically three main ways to think of how we express gratitude to others:

- Verbal gratitude: using speech to share words of thanks
- Concrete gratitude: giving a gift
- Connective gratitude: an act of kindness and friendship

Research by Jonathan Tudge, a professor at the University of North Carolina at Greensboro and an expert on cultural differences in gratitude, published a series of studies in 2017 examining how gratitude develops in children across seven very different countries: the United States, Brazil, Guatemala, Turkey, Russia, China, and South Korea. Naturally, there were similarities and differences. For example, as all children got older, they were less likely to respond with concrete gratitude. They also found:

- Children in China and South Korea favored connective gratitude
- Children in the United States favored concrete gratitude
- And as children in the United States, China, and Brazil grew older, they expressed more connective gratitude[4]

The research on grattude has grown exponentially, particularly in the last ten years, and while the work continues, even taking a quick peek at the research to date is fascinating.

We can honor how different cultures practice gratitude while simultaneously appreciating that cultures are dynamic, and variability among people is so great that focusing on any one thing would be too narrow of a lens. As shared earlier, culture is only one factor that shapes who we are. However, we can be aware and responsive as we develop relationships and celebrate diversity with our unique and dynamic learners.

Honoring How Peers Are Unique and Dynamic

Joshua Stamper is an administrator, author, and podcaster, and as I got to know him, I immediately noticed that he is someone who is very intentional in honoring what makes each person special, both kids and adults.

Gratitude through Love Languages

by Joshua Stamper
Administrator, Author, and Podcaster
Frisco, Texas

Over the years, I have heard several common statements from teachers, including "I don't know how much longer I can take the stress" and "I'm just so overwhelmed." As a campus leader, it's really tough to hear that your staff is struggling with many aspects of the job. In a profession that is established through purpose and love, it's hard to continue to serve when you are not feeling supported, validated, and valued.

Several years ago, my principal and I saw our staff becoming burned out. We were challenging them continually to be innovative in their practices, and they were working extremely hard to meet our goals. With the new initiatives, the teachers began to feel overwhelmed and underappreciated. Although our administrative team thought we were providing a lot of verbal praise to the staff, the perception from the majority of teachers was that their hard efforts were not validated. We knew something had to change immediately to improve our campus culture.

At the same time, I discovered *The 5 Languages of Appreciation in the Workplace*, by Gary Chapman, an interesting book on how people share and receive their gratitude and love in different ways. The book explored how appreciation can be demonstrated through words of affirmation, quality time, acts of service, tangible gifts, and physical touch, and explained how to incorporate these in an organization.[5]

Our first step was to understand that people receive encouragement and appreciation in multiple ways, and then to find out how each staff member valued receiving gratitude. To do so, we constructed a staff survey. As we surveyed our teachers, we found that it was difficult for some of our staff members to assess their own needs and how they enjoyed receiving gratitude, and a small percentage defaulted to choosing *words of affirmation* as their love language. Based on the results, we created a staff inventory that included the category of appreciation that each person had selected. As we worked on finding new ways to praise our staff, three important concepts stood out.

Intentional and Personal

In the past, providing praise was a spontaneous endeavor. As someone left my office, or when I passed someone in the hall, I would tell them they were doing an amazing job and how I appreciated everything they were doing. It was a nice gesture, but honestly, it had minimal impact. We knew we had to do better. Creating a staff appreciation inventory forced us to be more specific and personal about how we showed our gratitude toward our staff.

Listen to Your Staff

It became apparent that some of the self-assessment selections made on the survey were incorrect. To find the correct love languages of our staff, we had to listen to the requests of our teachers. Here are a few examples of teacher requests we observed that allowed us to determine if they enjoyed words of affirmation, quality time, acts of service, tangible gifts, or physical touch.

- "If you go to Sonic, will you pick up a sweet tea for me too?" (tangible gifts)
- "Does this lesson plan look all right?" (words of affirmation)
- "Do you want to meet in my room to work on the assessment together?" (quality time)
- "Will you make some copies for me and pick up some colored paper from the front office?" (acts of service)
- "I haven't seen you all day! How are you?" followed by a hug. (physical touch)

Of course, not every request determined the way each individual always enjoyed receiving gratitude. However, when we listened to teachers consistently, we began to find the trend in how they wanted to be appreciated.

You Can't Do This Alone

As a leader, it is easy to want to be the solution to a slipping campus culture. Personalizing gratitude schoolwide to staff is an extremely large job. We trained our leadership team so they were able to assist in the creation of the survey, the collection for the inventory, the budget for gifts and services, and the implementation of showing gratitude to our teachers.

By the end of the school year, we had seen an improvement in our staff morale, and many of the teachers commented on how they felt more appreciated—because we had individualized our appreciation. Regardless of how you show gratitude, make sure you are making an effort to connect with each staff member to understand what they need to feel loved.

Reflecting on Gratitude with Peers

Gratitude for our peers doesn't always come naturally, but it is critical that we make the effort to appreciate and support each other. Reflect on the current or most recent school year, and go through the notice-think-feel-do process discussed in chapter 2:

- Notice: What has gone well that we can be grateful for?
- Think: Why did we have these successes? Who contributed?
- Feel: How do we feel about these successes?
- Do: What can we do to show our appreciation?

You can write or sketch it in the space provided.

When it comes to the *do*, expressing gratitude, it doesn't have to be an overly elaborate gesture. In fact, a principal recently shared with me that she takes a pad of Post-it notes with her as she makes her rounds on campus. As she walks through classrooms, she makes a quick note about something she appreciates the teacher doing and leaves it on their desk. She loved doing it so much that she started leaving them for kids as well, and families have shared that their child's Post-it can be found in a highly visible place in the house, like the refrigerator, so all can see. It takes very little time, but this genuine act can have a huge impact.

Note: This principal has already established a school culture where teachers know that unscheduled walk-throughs are nonevaluative, and her team knows that if she places a Post-it down, it is a positive. If you decide to adopt a practice like this, be sure to lay the groundwork ahead of time. We wouldn't want a teacher to be midlesson and suffer a panic attack thinking they had done something that was not appreciated.

Gratitude with the World

> *Gratitude is the inward feeling of kindness received. Thankfulness is the natural impulse to express that feeling. Thanksgiving is the following of that impulse.*
>
> —Henry van Dyke

Kindness and Gratitude

The connection between kindness and gratitude in our world is significant and undeniable, but we don't always take the time to think about how the two are connected. Both are contagious and benefit all involved. You can find both in places you don't expect, and together kindness and gratitude can create a loop of positivity that makes us more resilient. Here is the story of how I became fully aware of the symbiotic relationship between kindness and gratitude and how it binds us as humans.

TOGETHER KINDNESS AND GRATITUDE CAN CREATE A LOOP OF POSITIVITY THAT MAKES US MORE RESILIENT.

It was Friday, December 14, 2012, and I was on the road facilitating professional learning with a group of educators. We were wrapping up our second day, and I was demonstrating ways to find and validate information on the internet using credible sources. I navigated to a news site and couldn't believe the headline, "Gunman Massacres Twenty Children at School in Connecticut." A shockwave of horror spread through the room. I remember driving to the airport later. I needed to get home to my then-two-year-old-daughter and hug her so tight. I was shaken, and my heart broke for the families and the educators. I did the only thing I could think of—I prayed for the Sandy Hook community.

Almost three years later, in August 2015, I received an email from a member of the Stratford Board of Education that started, "Today, we officially opened a very special school, Victoria Soto School." The message went on to explain that Victoria Soto was a heroic Sandy Hook teacher who hid her first graders from the shooter and was shot when she used her body to shield her students. In 2013, she was posthumously awarded the Presidential Citizen's Medal, and now this K–2 school in the next town was opening in her honor.

The email went on to ask if I could provide professional learning and coaching for the teachers on effective ways to leverage technology for learning. I'm embarrassed to say I had mixed emotions. I'm always excited to start a new collaboration, but, if I'm being totally honest, I was afraid this community would harbor a lot of sadness, and selfishly, I wasn't sure I could handle it. It had been almost three years, yet I was still shaken, and I lived on the other side of the country and had no direct connection to the community. I am so thankful I got over myself, because I learned so much about resilience, kindness, and gratitude through this community.

My first day on campus I was given a tour, and what I experienced was so touching. The campus was so vibrant, and I could hear the laughter of kinder, first, and second graders as soon as I walked through the front doors. Teachers wore smiles, genuinely happy to be there. My tour guide explained that the physical school was designed to honor Victoria Soto in as many ways as possible. The walls and hallways were painted with bright green and blue, which were Victoria's favorite colors. In the courtyard were ministatues of pink flamingos in honor of Victoria's favorite animal and, as an added touch, each classroom had a single flamingo-pink chair for the teacher. In the central corridor was the best tribute of all, a giant mosaic of tiles that spelled out *be kind*. It was a simple message, but one that was so powerful I had a visceral reaction.

After my first day of being in classrooms working with kids and teachers, one of the teachers called me back to her room. She explained that her students had something for me. I walked into the room unsure of what it would be when a soft-spoken first grader presented me with what he called a *kindness coin* for spending the day with them and teaching them. It was a colorful, handcrafted, ceramic flower the size of a coin, and it hung on a chain that you wear around your neck. He explained that you don't keep kindness coins; you need to pass them on to others who display kindness. You catch someone doing something good and thank them by awarding them the kindness coin. Then, the next day, it is the job of the person wearing the kindness coin to catch someone else being kind. They shared several examples:

- Malik, for always pushing in everyone's chair before recess.
- Samantha, for letting Hayden join in the handball game.
- Mateo, for helping other classmates even when he isn't finished with his own stuff.
- Aidan, for always being kind to his tablemates.

Expressing as much gratitude as I could while also fighting back tears of appreciation, I asked if I could take the kindness coin to California and pass it on to students there. They loved the idea, so I connected the Connecticut class to a class in Southern California, and the two classes exchanged their stories through letters, emails, and videos for the remainder of the school year. (Even if you don't have a connection to a teacher somewhere else in the world, there are a number of free services that safely connect classrooms with each other.) As you can imagine, kindness and gratitude were interwoven in all of the exchanges, and both the kids and the teachers found tremendous joy from the experience.

Knowing what Victoria Soto did to protect her first graders, I can only imagine the paradox of emotions that the Soto family feels having this learning community dedicated to her. At the opening of the school, Victoria's father, Carlos Soto said, "From something ugly, something beautiful has come."[1] What a profound message.

I learned so much from this community, and I will never forget the way they share kindness and gratitude. I'm also incredibly grateful to the teacher at Victoria Soto School and the teacher in California who partnered with each other to collaborate. Two schools, thousands of miles away, yet connected by kindness and gratitude.

Public Displays of Gratitude

Public displays of gratitude can go well beyond the basic thank-you, giving much more depth to the expression. After all, when you want to share your appreciation for someone, it can be really fun letting everyone know about it! For example, when I write letters of gratitude, I don't fold them up and hide them in an envelope. No way! I print them on cardstock and frame them for all to see. Plus, gratitude is contagious so the more who see it, the more the gratitude spreads.

In his book *Because of a Teacher: Stories of the Past to Inspire the Future of Education*, George Couros invited educators to share their stories about teachers and administrators who have made an impact. It's a book filled with open letters of gratitude, and I had the extraordinary opportunity to contribute by writing about Dr. Monique Huibregtse, an administrator who changed my life. The idea of writing it felt like a public practice of deep reflection and gratitude. I feel joy just thinking about it, and I had never written anything with such ease.

Because of a Teacher

by George Couros

**Innovative Teaching, Learning, and
Leadership Consultant
Edmonton, Alberta, Canada**

Like it did on the rest of the world, March
2020 had a significant impact on my life and the lives of those
around me. As someone who benefited from traveling around the
globe and working with educators, I quickly had to figure out a
new path. I was nervous about what the future would hold and
how the change in my career would affect me and my family.

One of the things that I had focused on in the years prior was
the practice of gratitude. I remember building on these two questions from Tim Denning and making a practice in my own life. He
had shared the following prompts:

1. Did I learn one new thing today?
2. Did I help or inspire one person?[2]

I loved the questions, but I wanted to add a third.

3. Did I show gratitude to someone who has had a positive
   impact on me?

I was going through these questions prior to March of 2020,
and I felt that it helped center me at the end of the day while setting the tone for the next.

But I let that practice slip away.

And then I remember reading a post by my good friend
Patrick Larkin titled "Never a Better Time to Practice Gratitude." I
read this quote and was a bit thrown off: "Find one thing each day
that you are grateful for that would not have been possible if we
were not in these unique circumstances. Parents, ask your children
to do the same."

My first thought was, "Wow . . . this feels really selfish!" When people were really struggling, trying to find good seemed to be a self-centered endeavor.[3]

But I know Patrick well, and I will tell you, he is one of the most caring and giving people I have ever met. So I gave him the benefit of the doubt, and at dinner, I asked my daughter Kallea, who was three at the time, "What is something you are grateful for?"

She looked at me and said, "Daddy home."

Single-tear moment.

I had been on the road for the past ten years without a month straight at home, and all of a sudden, her words helped me recalibrate and focus on what I *did* have at the moment versus what I didn't. Taking that inward focus on what I was grateful for all of a sudden helped me think about how I could help others. What had felt like a selfish act had truly helped me become selfless in my focus.

I noticed this two-week period in the world where educators were celebrated for their fantastic work during COVID-19, and I felt people finally appreciated schools and teachers for all they had done for our communities. But then those two weeks seemed to end, and I not only saw a lack of appreciation but, in some cases, vitriol toward educators. I know that many people were dealing with stressful situations, but it truly hurt my heart. I decided I wanted to make a difference and help change the narrative, so I started a series called *Three Questions on Educators That Inspire* on my podcast that would ask the following:

Who is a teacher that inspired you?

Who is an administrator that inspired you?

What advice would you give to your first-year teacher-self?

This was a way to share the excellent practices of educators and show gratitude for the teachers that made an impact on our lives. I wanted to model the practice, so I answered these questions first and talked about three of my teachers. My kindergarten teacher, my music teachers, and my high school football coach. I shared heartfelt stories of them, and within forty-eight hours, each one reached out to me to thank me for the acknowledgment! I had not talked to two of them in probably over twenty years, but here they were, cheering me on and thanking me for taking the time to acknowledge them!

I thought about how many educators in the world had no idea of their impact on students. They will never get the thank-yous they deserve, but if I could get them one closer, that is at least a good start.

That podcast series turned into a book titled *Because of a Teacher*, where fifteen educators shared their answers to these questions. The coauthors of this book wrote incredible stories and, in many cases, I saw them giving copies of the book to the teachers they had written about, and it truly warmed my heart. The hope was not just to highlight our great teachers but to encourage others in and out of the profession, in some way, to reach out to their former teachers and let them know about their impact. It has been magical to watch that practice of gratitude for others not only spread across the world, but also reach back in time to let teachers know their impact.

It has also been beautiful to watch as several schools started their own podcast with their current students to ask them about a teacher that has impacted them. Not only does this share what resonates with our kids, but also it encourages students not to wait forty years, like I did, to let their teachers know the impact they have had on them!

I always say this and do my best to embody it: It is always better to share gratitude for others *too early* rather than *too late*. It is a selfless act that benefits not only those who receive it but also those who give it.

That third question that George added, "Did I show gratitude to someone who has had a positive impact on me?" is simple yet essential. *Because of a Teacher* is filled with stories of profound gratitude, but if you really think about it, each and every day many people have a positive impact on us. The next time you go to the grocery store and see those stocked shelves, think of how many people it took to make that possible—the farmers, the factory workers, the truck drivers, and the grocery store workers to name a few. Thanks to these people, my family and I are nourished with very little effort on our part. And while we don't always get to know everyone involved, we do connect with some of these hard-working people. We can learn their names, thank them, and take a little extra time to also publicly thank them for their efforts in an online business review. Think about all the services that you use in your life and all the opportunities to publicly show gratitude for those people: health-care workers, sales people, food servers, hairdressers, house cleaners, food-delivery drivers, mechanics, and rideshare drivers just to name a few. You could make someone's day and also feel great about yourself for putting a little positivity out into the world.

Professionally, I also think about ways to thank content creators such as authors and podcasters for sharing their ideas and stretching my thinking. I must admit, before my first book was published, I didn't really think about how vulnerable and exposed I would feel as an author. You share your work, but what if no one likes it? (I still get anxious putting content out there, but I've learned to keep going!) For years, I never thought much of that email from Amazon asking me to write a review for a recently purchased book. Now, I write a glowing review for every book and every podcast that makes me better. I also share it on social media tagging the content creator. I think I'm pretty darn good at doing this, but Stephanie Rothstein takes it to a whole new level! Plus, Steph's #WalkRead practice is an amazing life hack. I think of it as *temptation bundling*, which is a strategy I learned about from Katy Milkman, PhD.[4] The idea is to combine one thing you should do, but often procrastinate on doing, with one thing that you can't wait to do. Here's how Steph uses temptation bundling with exercise, learning, and gratitude.

#WalkRead, Share Out, and Hug That Book

by Stephanie Rothstein
Educator, Mentor, and Writer
San Jose, California

I began my practice of #WalkRead in the spring of 2020. It helped me to get outside and get moving, and that quiet provided me the space to focus and dive deep into books. I received lots of interested looks from neighbors and lots of questions about walking and reading at the same time. To help give you an idea of how it works: I take the same route around my local park, bring the physical book, and walk on the sidewalk. I even bought a special neck lamp for the journey. I realized quickly that it had to be books I wanted to devour, and I absolutely love reading books on educational leadership—there's nothing better than hearing an author's voice through their writing. I never thought of what I was doing as a practice of gratitude. But, it has certainly become this. For me, reading the words of others, thinking deeply about their ideas, and applying it to my own work is in itself an act of gratitude. I am grateful to those who continue to put their words into the world and share their insight.

But keeping this for myself wasn't enough; I needed a way to express their impact on me and show appreciation. Thank you, Twitter! Social media allowed me to share 280 characters about each book, point out three to four specific takeaways, and connect with others on topics of interest. It became my routine and my practice. I was surprised at how much these short reflections resonated with others. Educators from around the world commented on specific parts from the book or quoted moments in the text that they connected with, leading us to have our own book-tweet discussion. As my reflection and connection process evolved, it grew to include articles and podcasts. I used Twitter and my blog to share my takeaways on all things I read or listened to that inspired me. I realized the importance of documenting my own learning journey and thanking those who have been part of it. Educators who put their words out there have no idea of the impact they make unless we tell them.

I learned from Adam Grant to normalize vulnerability, from Sean Gaillard that courageous collaboration "starts with an invitation," from Dr. Katie Martin that "it isn't about doing more, it's about doing different," from George Couros that "we should not only learn how to survive change but thrive through the process," from Lauren Kaufman that "eventually, signposts in the roads will appear, offering a new direction to creation, development, and growth," and from Meghan Lawson that "I don't need to be perfect . . . My job is to keep going. My job is to keep trying."

Their words changed me for the better. I was inspired to keep learning, growing, and sharing. The more I did this, the more it connected me with the authors and other educators, and grew my personal learning network. There is a power to sharing the impact that others' words have had on you. Sharing privately is meaningful, and I have written private messages of gratitude to many authors, but there is also a power to letting other educators in on our insights and journeys. Hearing the perspectives of others enriches the conversation and extends the learning. Isn't that the reason these authors share their voices in the first place? I am grateful to each of them. It is the reason I hug books so tight. I feel connected to these brilliant people through their writing; their voices continue to inspire me. I will never stop sharing my learning and gratitude with the world, and I know I am better because of them.

Using social media platforms that are designed for sharing makes amplifying gratitude even easier. This is also a great way to highlight folks who do so much in our learning communities but don't always get acknowledged. Think about your custodians, office manager, paraprofessionals, etc. You can include photos, graphics, and video to complement the text and make the post more visually engaging. Tag news outlets that might appreciate a human interest story. You never know where a small act of gratitude could take you. And this next story is a perfect example of never knowing where gratitude can lead.

#GratitudeSnaps

by Tara Martin and Tisha Richmond
Educators and Authors
Kansas and Oregon

Tisha remembers the conversation like it was yesterday. It was a summer day in 2017, and she was talking on the phone with her soul sister, Tara Martin, who was struggling with feelings of inadequacy, frustration, and low self-worth. It broke Tisha's heart to hear the internal struggle in Tara's voice. Her negative thoughts were

spiraling into a deep, dark place, and Tisha desperately wanted to pull her out.

As Tara shared, Tisha kept thinking about times when she was in a similar place. Life is a roller coaster of ups, downs, twists, and turns that can bring us joyful highs and devastating lows. For Tisha, reflecting on the pivotal moments that have marked her journey brings hope and courage to face what lies ahead. Though Tisha could see all of Tara's past amazing accomplishments and positive things happening in her life so clearly, Tara couldn't.

In a desperate attempt to help her precious friend, Tisha suggested a thirty-day gratitude journal as a possible solution. It wasn't more than two seconds after this suggestion left her lips that she had an even better idea! "Tara, what about creating #GratitudeSnaps! Rather than keeping a journal, you could snap a daily picture of something you are grateful for, make a snap out of it, and then share it out via social media! This would allow you to express yourself in a way that you love and focus on the positives in your life! Just as #BookSnaps helps connect and draw meaning from text, #GratitudeSnaps could help connect with the positive in your life in a meaningful way."

Of course, Tara thought Tisha's idea of #GratitudeSnaps was brilliant! But, as Tara considered creating her own gratitude journal, she immediately wondered if, like they had with #BookSnaps, they might take this global. Surely Tara is not the only one that battles low moments quietly. The idea was for everyone to post #GratitudeSnaps daily during the month of November and flood social media with positivity!

You see, what Tisha didn't know at the time was that every year at the end of October, the anniversary of her father's murder haunts Tara. Her traumatic childhood runs deep, and specific times of the year are more difficult than others. While Tisha could see the outward behaviors and expressions of "feelings of inadequacy, frustration, and low self-worth," she wasn't fully aware of the root cause.

Tara has a very creative mind, and it's incredible when it flows productively. But when it goes dark, it's like a multilane highway jammed, bumper-to-bumper with negative traffic. However, an interesting thing happened as she created #GratitudeSnaps—exits were created!

Yes, gratitude reroutes the mind!

Isn't it wild that gratefulness can literally rewire our brains?

As others joined in around the world sharing #GratitudeSnaps, Tara and Tisha's empathy levels increased. Not only did this challenge increase their own serotonin levels, but also everyone else benefited from practicing thankfulness openly and seeing the beautiful things others were intentionally posting, too. The ripple effect was, and continues to be, immeasurable!

Who knew that a heartfelt phone conversation between friends would inspire an annual movement reaching around the globe. Intentionally reframing our perspective through the lens of a grateful heart allows us to illuminate the joy in our daily lives and share it with others. Joy is contagious. Think about how bright and beautiful our world would be if we all were able to share just a little joy each day.

Maybe we don't know what those around us are going through, but we can provide tools to help—just as Tisha did that day.

#GratitudeSnaps—it just might be the tool that allows your learners to create exits within their minds and free up mental space for learning and productivity.

Want to join the #GratitudeSnaps Challenge?

Each day during the month of November, simply post a picture of something for which you are grateful and share it on social media using the hashtag #GratitudeSnaps. It could be a thing, a person, a feeling, etc.; it's personal to you. Any picture app can be used to create them. Learn more from our blogs: tarammartin.com/gratitudesnaps-challenge-2021 and tisharichmond.com/blog/gratitudesnaps-2021. Also, be sure to tag us @TaraMartinEDU and @tishrich on Twitter.

We invite everyone to join the #GratitudeSnaps Challenge. Let's flood the world with gratefulness!

Our Legacy for the Greater Good

> *Do your little bit of good where you are; it's those little bits of good put together that overwhelm the world.*
>
> **—Desmond Tutu**

As educators we have the unique honor and power of shaping the future. Brianna Henneke Hodges is an educator and a strategic storyteller sharing how gratitude and story can be part of our legacy. As you read Bri's story, I encourage you to ask yourself, What will the story of your gratitude legacy be?

Stories of Gratitude: Our Legacy

by Brianna Henneke Hodges

Education Consultant and Strategic Storyteller
Stephenville, Texas

When we declare and express our gratitude, we're, in fact, telling a story.

Stories are our way to say thank you to our world.

My parents believed the act and art of writing thank-you letters to be a significant part of my (and my brother's) character development. Regardless of the gift's value, we wrote a fairly detailed narrative of the gift's impact.

Now, I'm not pretending that I always approached these letters as an opportunity instead of a chore, but, taking the time to lean into the spirit of gratitude and acknowledging the person or people behind the present instilled within me that gifts and gratitude are recursively hand-in-hand and symbiotic.

To receive a thoughtful gift and to share genuine appreciation for that gesture by way of a written narrative paved the way for the next iteration of gratitude: the lasting connection of story.

Including the required details forced us to move from a focus on the item to recognition of intent and celebration of impact. This meant we couldn't summarily say thanks. Instead, we had to reflect on why we were grateful and how we saw the gift positively shaping our worlds. There were times when this task was particularly challenging (most especially during my angsty teen years). Nonetheless, the challenge of looking beyond the surface to find true gratitude proved to be the ultimate outcome my parents were after.

Without a doubt, it is decidedly different, and even difficult, to find presents amid pain and problems. These camouflaged gifts—the ones that hide in deep cover, forcing us to squint super hard—are honey holes of gratitude, as they help us see the hope within the overwhelm, the possibility amid the impossible.

I've taken my parents' lesson and teach it now to my own children. In fact, I taught it in my classroom and as a district leader as well, taking care to show my thanks in detail for the *why* and in appreciation for the *how*. No matter the appearance, we honor the greater impact when we share stories of thanks, and we transform influence into legacy when we share stories of gratitude.

Empowering Learners with Purpose

Work and live to serve others, to leave the world a little better than you found it and garner for yourself as much peace of mind as you can. This is happiness.
—David Sarnoff

When we think about everything going on in the world—the exploitation, oppression, and violence—whether we're experiencing it or feeling powerless to change it, those thoughts can flood us with sorrow and make it difficult to think about our story of gratitude. As discussed in chapter 2, we are wired with negativity bias, so we do need to pay extra attention to the good, but there are real challenges in the world that can't be ignored. Thankfully, our legacy as educators can be one of cultivating grateful learners and empowering them with purpose. So how do we activate our grateful learners as agents of change?

Prosocial behavior is defined as behavior intended to help other people. There are inquiry-driven pedagogical methods that are learner driven and have the capacity to promote prosocial behavior.[5] For example, design thinking, project-based learning (PBL), and challenge-based learning (CBL) can be effective learning frameworks that offer space to think about what we are grateful for and use that to design prosocial learning experiences that solve real-world problems. As we practice gratitude with kids, we can use their individual stories of gratitude to create a road map for how we can turn our gratitude into prosocial action. For example, when kids share that they are grateful for nourishing food at school, they can work with custodians and cafeteria workers to collect food waste for a compost bin. They can also tend a campus garden and use the crops in cooking classes or donate the produce to a local food bank. There are so many opportunities for prosocial learning!

Working with adolescents, we have even more opportunities to get out into the community for prosocial learning. Service learning has been around for decades, and we can leverage these experiences as opportunities to cultivate gratitude.

- Gratitude for local history can lead to working with senior citizens to create a local cultural journal that reports on the unique aspects of the community.
- Gratitude for learning can lead to tutoring children in underserved areas on subjects such as math and reading, which deepens the tutor's understanding of content.
- Gratitude for physical education and health can lead to conducting sports clinics for a variety of athletics.

We can empower our kids to be agents of change who make the world a better place. Kids can experience and express gratitude as purpose-driven, contributing members of society and we, as educators, will be better for it, too.

PROSOCIAL LEARNING

Grateful for...	Learners...
food that nourishes us	work with custodians and cafeteria workers to collect food waste for a compost bin; tend the campus garden
technology to amplify learning	create content to educate the world; purposeful work that is shared online to help many
our bodies and being alive	educate families about healthy living and develop a plan for healthy habits (diet, sleep, & fitness)
our community	identify ways to have a positive impact on their community; implement and measure their level of success

Could gratitude combined with learner-driven practices be the catalyst for positive transformation in our learning communities and the worldwide community at large? I believe it is.

CONCLUSION

Give a Shout-Out

I've come to believe that living in a state of gratitude is the gateway to grace.
—Arianna Huffington

As George Couros shared in his story, "It is always better to share gratitude for others *too early* rather than *too late*." I also think about Dan Pink's book *The Power of Regret: How Looking Backward Moves Us Forward*, where he shares the difference between action vs. inaction regrets and the fact that, as we age, inaction regrets increase. In other words, what we really regret are the things we didn't do.[1]

We don't need to have regrets about gratitude. The time to develop and nurture a grateful disposition is now! Taking James Clear's advice shared in chapter 2, we should focus on consistency rather than intensity. So who are you ready to give a shout-out to?

In the video "Give a Shout-Out," by SoulPancake, their street team places a ginormous microphone on a bustling sidewalk with a simple sign that invites people to give a shout-out to the people who matter to them. Those who stop are heard saying things like:

- "Shout-out to my friends for making my life a little easier during these rough moments."
- "To my wife for putting up with my crazy self."
- "I was in a continuation high school, not really caring about my life, and a man named Robert Gillio taught me how to dance. It is my career now, and if it wasn't for that, I don't know where I'd be."[2]

We don't often pass by a huge microphone and a call to action like this, but we always have the opportunity to express gratitude. So what are we waiting for? If you like, I'll go first!

Thank you to you for taking time from your busy schedule to read this book. Your commitment to experiencing and expressing gratitude will have untold ripple effects making your life and the lives of those around you better.

If you use social media, please consider amplifying your stories of gratitude using the hashtag #EvolvingWithGratitude. Together we can use these small practices to make a big impact with kids, peers, and the world. Let's start now!

Resources We Can Be Grateful For

In addition to the important works referenced throughout the book, here are some extra gratitude resources.

Read:

Gratitude Is My Superpower: A Children's Book about Giving Thanks and Practicing Positivity by Alicia Ortego

Lead with Appreciation: Fostering a Culture of Gratitude by Amber Teamann and Melinda Miller

The Little Book of Gratitude: Create a Life of Happiness and Wellbeing by Giving Thanks by Dr. Robert Emmons

"Savoring in Psychology: 21 Exercises and Interventions to Appreciate Life" by Daniela Ramirez, PhD, at PositivePsychology .com

Watch:

"The Gratitude Experiment" by WellCast on YouTube.com

"Want to Be Happy? Be Grateful" by Brother David Steindl-Rast on TED.com

Listen:

"Grateful Expectations," episode 2 of *The Happiness Lab* podcast with Laurie Santos

"How Gratitude Benefits Your Brain," episode 7 of *The Science of Happiness* podcast by the Greater Good Science Center

"Adam Grant on Rethinking," an April 2021 episode of *What I've Learned with Arianna Huffington*

"Six-Minute Guided Gratitude Contemplation" by Kelly McGonigal on kellymcgonigal.com/gratitude

Explore:

"Greater Good in Action:" Gratitude practices available at greatergood.berkeley.edu

Thnx4!: A gratitude journaling website available at thnx4.org

Notes

Introduction

1   Collaborative for Academic, Social, and Emotional Learning (CASEL), accessed March 14, 2022, casel.org/fundamentals-of-sel/.

2   Marc A. Brackett, *Permission to Feel: Unlocking the Power of Emotions to Help Our Kids, Ourselves, and Our Society Thrive* (New York, NY: Celadon Books, 2019).

3   Brené Brown, "Regret Is a Fair but Tough Teacher," *Oprah*, 2015. oprah.com/own-super-soul-sunday/brene-brown-regret-is-a-fair-but-tough-teacher-video.

4   Jay Shetty, *Think Like a Monk: Train Your Mind for Peace and Purpose Every Day* (New York, NY: Simon & Schuster, 2020).

Chapter 1

1   Courtney E. Ackerman, "What Is Gratitude and Why Is It So Important?" *PositivePsychology*, January 9, 2020, positivepsychology.com/gratitude-appreciation/.

2   Summer Allen, "The Science of Gratitude," Greater Good Science Center, 2018, ggsc.berkeley.edu/images/uploads/GGSC-JTF_White_Paper-Gratitude-FINAL.pdf.

3   Jeremy Adam Smith, Dacher Keltner, Jason Marsh, and Kira M. Newman, *The Gratitude Project: How Cultivating Thankfulness Can Rewire Your Brain for Resilience, Optimism, and the Greater Good* (Oakland, CA: New Harbinger Publications, 2020).

4   Robert A. Emmons, *Thanks!: How the New Science of Gratitude Can Make You Happier* (Boston, MA: Houghton Mifflin Co., 2007).

5   Brené Brown, *Atlas of the Heart: Mapping Meaningful Connection and the Language of Human Experience* (New York, NY: Random House, 2022).

Chapter 2

1   Laura Kelly Fanucci, "When This Is Over," Instagram post, March 16, 2020, instagram.com/p/B9zCs-xl3x2.

2   Catherine Moore, "What Is Negativity Bias and How Can It Be Overcome?" *PositivePsychology*, December 30, 2019, positivepsychology .com/3-steps-negativity-bias/.

3   Steven Pinker, "Is the World Getting Better or Worse? A Look at the Numbers," TED Talk, 2018, ted.com/talks/steven_pinker_is_the_world _getting_better_or_worse_a_look_at_the_numbers.

4   Madhuleena Roy Chowdhury, "The Neuroscience of Gratitude and How It Affects Anxiety & Grief," *PositivePsychology*, January 9, 2020, positivepsychology.com/neuroscience-of-gratitude/.

5   Mitchel Adler and Nancy Fagley, "Gratitude Quiz," Greater Good Magazine, accessed March 14, 2022, greatergood.berkeley.edu/quizzes/ take_quiz/gratitude.

6   Jeremy Adam Smith, Dacher Keltner, Jason Marsh, and Kira M. Newman, *The Gratitude Project: How Cultivating Thankfulness Can Rewire Your Brain for Resilience, Optimism, and the Greater Good* (Oakland, CA: New Harbinger Publications, 2020).

7   "Oprah's Gratitude Journal," *Oprah's Lifeclass*, 2012, oprah.com/oprahs -lifeclass/oprah-on-the-importance-of-her-gratitude-journal-video.

8   Andrew Huberman, "The Science of Gratitude & How to Build a Gratitude Practice," *Huberman Lab*, podcast, November 22, 2021, hubermanlab.com/the-science-of-gratitude-and-how-to-build-a -gratitude-practice/.

9   Glenn R. Fox, Jonas Kaplan, Hanna Damasio, and Antonio Damasio, "Neural Correlates of Gratitude," *Frontiers in Psychology* 6 (2015), doi.org/10.3389/fpsyg.2015.01491.

10   Louie Schwartzberg, "Nature. Beauty. Gratitude," TED Talk, 2011, ted.com/talks/louie_schwartzberg_nature_beauty_gratitude.

11   Regina Brett, *God Never Blinks: 50 Lessons for Life's Little Detours* (New York, NY: Grand Central Publishing, 2011).

12   Andrea Hussong, "How to Practice Gratitude? Notice. Think. Feel. Do." *Dynamic Minds*, blog, the University of North Carolina at Chapel Hill, November 24, 2020, unc.edu/discover/how-to-practice-gratitude -notice-think-feel-do/.

13 "Admiral McRaven Addresses the University of Texas at Austin Class of 2014," YouTube video, the University of Texas at Austin, 2014, youtube .com/watch?v=yaQZFhrW0fU.

14 "SEL 3 Signature Practices Playbook: Practical Ways to Introduce and Broaden the Use of SEL Practices in Classrooms, Schools, and Workplaces," Collaborative for Academic, Social, and Emotional Learning (CASEL), 2013.

15 Carol Dweck, *Mindset: Changing the Way You Think to Fulfil Your Potential* (London: Robinson, 2017).

Chapter 3

1 "Emotion revolution—student," Yale Center for Emotional Intelligence, 2015, ei.yale.edu/what-we-do/emotion-revolution-student/.

2 Kerry Howells, "How Thanking Awakens Our Thinking," TED Talk, 2013, m.youtube.com/watch?v=gzfhPB_NtVc.

3 "Universal Design for Learning Guidelines Version 2.2," graphic organizer, CAST, 2018, udlguidelines.cast.org/.

4 "Community of Inquiry," adapted from Garrison and Anderson (2003), University of Toronto, 2016, teaching.utoronto.ca/wp-content/ uploads/2016/05/Community-of-Inquiry.pdf.

5 Jeffrey J. Froh and Giacomo Bono, *Making Grateful Kids: The Science of Building Character* (West Conshohocken, PA: Templeton Press, 2014).

6 Lainie Rowell, "Cultivating a Culture of Authentic Gratitude," Edutopia, August 20, 2021, edutopia.org/article/cultivating-culture-authentic -gratitude.

Chapter 4

1 Elizabeth D. Steiner and Ashley Woo, "Job-Related Stress Threatens the Teacher Supply: Key Findings from the 2021 State of the U.S. Teacher Survey," RAND Corporation, 2021, rand.org/pubs/research_reports/ RRA1108-1.html.

2 "Gratitude Curricula," Greater Good Science Center, 2022, ggsc.berkeley.edu/who_we_serve/educators/educator_resources/ gratitude_curricula.

3 Katie Martin, "The Science of Happiness: 3 Practices That Changed My Perspective," *Katielmartin.com*, blog, April 21, 2019,

katielmartin.com/2019/04/21/the-science-of-happiness-3-pratices-that
-changed-my-perspective/.

4   Kira M. Newman, "How Cultural Differences Shape Your Gratitude,"
Greater Good Magazine July 15, 2019, greatergood.berkeley.edu/article/
item/how_cultural_differences_shape_your_gratitude.

5   G. D. Chapman and P. E. White, *The 5 Languages of Appreciation in the
Workplace: Empowering Organizations by Encouraging People* (Chicago,
IL: Northfield Publishing, 2019).

Chapter 5

1   Catalina Trivino and Ari Mason, "Victoria Soto School Opens in
Stratford," *NBCconnecticut,* August 28, 2015, nbcconnecticut.com/news/
local/victoria-soto-school-opens-in-stratford/88940/.

2   Tim Denning, "The Most Important Way to Measure Your Day," June
13, 2019, medium.com/the-ascent/the-most-important-way-to-measure
-your-day-e43a8a042b63.

3   Patrick Larkin, "Never a Better Time to Practice #Gratitude," March 17,
2020, patrickmlarkin.blog/2020/03/17/never-a-better-time-to
-practice-gratitude/.

4   K. L., Milkman, J. A. Minson, and K. G. Volpp, "Holding the Hunger
Games Hostage at the Gym: An Evaluation of Temptation Bundling,"
Management Science 60 (2014): 299.

5   Kendra Cherry, "The Basics of Prosocial Behavior," *Verywell Mind,*
October 13, 2020, verywellmind.com/what-is-prosocial-behavior
-2795479.

Conculsion

1   Daniel H. Pink, *The Power of Regret: How Looking Backward Moves Us
Forward* (New York, NY: Riverhead Books, 2022).

2   SoulPancake Street Team, "Give a Shout Out," YouTube video, 2013,
youtube.com/watch?v=lVqsKGqYgkY&t=7s.

With Thanks

In my first book, *Evolving Learner*, my portion of the acknowledgments section was so long that one of the editors kindly (and with the best of intentions) pointed out that there are other ways to thank the countless people I appreciate. And while this is true, I don't regret taking up that real estate in the book to show gratitude. In fact, I'd like to continue it here, and I'm going to start with those I know I don't show enough gratitude to: my first-and-forever teachers, my parents. I couldn't possibly thank them for everything, so I'll focus on some of the ways I believe they made me a grateful person.

Thank you to my mom, the most positive person on the planet and a professional cheerleader (figuratively and literally having been a Charger Girl). She has been my cheerleader long after she retired her pom-poms, and she is always a phone call away when I need support. A strong, hard-working professional, she sees challenges as opportunities to learn. She personifies gratitude in countless ways. I remember going on camping trips when I was growing up, and she taught me how to clean a stack of dirty dishes using very little water. Moments like this made me grateful for the little things that are actually big things, like clean water flowing from the tap (which I still turn off as soon as I'm finished thanks to her).

Thank you to my dad, the most generous person I know. A man who grew up on a homestead in Alaska and should have a scarcity mindset but never complains about growing up lacking things. In fact, the nearest grocery store was more than five hundred miles away, but his memories focus on how there was always plenty of salmon, king crab, clams, caribou, and moose to eat. His life after the homestead also fascinates me. He served in the military and was a race car driver. During my childhood, he was an international pilot, and the tremendous lengths he went through to get home to us between trips is astounding. Clearly, he is incredibly hard-working, but he also has the sharpest wit, and he is always making me laugh. My dad is very humble, so I want to thank my stepmom, who helps me pull the stories out of him.

Thank you to my husband, who supports me when I have crazy ideas like writing another book. I can still see the look on his face when I said I was going to write this book, and I'm thankful for his quick recovery. It only took him a few seconds to wipe away the surprise (and concern) and put a smile on his face. From that moment on, not only did he support my decision, he encouraged me every step of the way as he always does. I don't know what I did to deserve such an amazing life partner, but I'm eternally grateful.

Thank you to my kids, who exponentially changed my life for the better. They join me in my daily gratitude practice, and the way they see the world with true awe inspires me to be even more thankful. Kendall has a pure heart and gets tremendous joy from helping others. Her teachers describe her as a spark in the classroom bringing her energy, engagement, and appreciation to the learning community, which makes her teacher-mom so proud. Blake is kind with a huge focus on family, spending time together, and making others laugh. Endlessly curious, he wants to learn everything about the world around him. He is always quick to offer me a hug, and I truly appreciate it.

Thank you to my in-laws, wow, I hit the jackpot here! They are truly the kindest, most humble people, and I'm honored to call them *family by choice.*

As I mentioned in the beginning of this book, I struggle with indebtedness. However, as I work to manage it, I have come to realize that we are truly connected as humans, and when you receive gifts from others, you can be indebted without feeling guilty. The contributors in this book gave me beautiful gifts; they are gifts to share with you and others. This helps me gladly, and without guilt, accept them.

Thank you to the entire IMPress team for supporting me through this process. A special thank you to George Couros for inspiring this book. He not only embodies gratefulness, but he also taught me the importance of articulating the value of gratitude out loud. He invited me to write a chapter for *Because of a Teacher*, and the joy I felt writing about my gratitude for Monique compelled me to write this. (Just one of the many positive ripple effects from *Because of a Teacher*.) Thank you to Paige Couros for being so encouraging, responsive, and all-around amazing! Thank you to the editorial team, in particular Lindsey Alexander, Salvatore Borriello, and Candida Hadley for handling authors' words with such care. I feel so blessed to work with the entire IMPress team.

Thank you to Allyson Liu, who is a lifelong friend and an immensely talented creative. I reached out to her as soon as I signed the contract for this book, and she had the cover designed before I had written the second chapter. She has the ability to take your ideas and make them even better than you dreamed they could be. Such a gift!

Thank you to Katie Novak, a true friend, the one who ignited my passion for writing often, and a constant inspiration. Thank you to Stephanie Rothstein, who cowrote my first Edutopia article with me and gave me the first nudge to write this book. Thank you to Sean Gaillard, for giving me the confidence to write this book. Thank you to Mandy Froehlich, who generously (and ironically) gave up part of her Thanksgiving break to review this book. She provided encouragement and essential feedback.

Thank you to Brianna Henneke Hodges, my podcast partner and dear friend; our passion project has been an amazing learning journey.

Thank you to Tom Berger, Marva Hinton, and the entire Edutopia team for helping me grow as a writer.

I see the fingerprints of everyone mentioned above throughout this book, and I'm overwhelmed with appreciation and joy.

I've been writing these acknowledgments since the inception of this book and it is, by far, the hardest part of the book to write because

I know I could go on forever. I have much more to say and many more people I want to thank, but I've reached a point where I'll take that *Evolving Learner* editor's advice. I'll continue my thanks in other ways, and I'll be sure to do it often.

Thank you to you for opening your heart and your mind to gratitude. I hope gratitude brings you as much joy as it has brought me.

With a heart full of thanks,
Lainie

About the Author

Lainie Rowell is an educator and international consultant. She is dedicated to building learning communities, and her areas of focus include learner-driven design, social-emotional learning, online and blended learning, and professional learning. During her twenty-five years as an educator, Lainie has taught elementary, secondary, and higher education. She also served in a district-level leadership position supporting twenty-two thousand students and twelve-hundred teachers at thirty-three schools.

As a consultant, Lainie's client list ranges from Fortune 100 companies like Apple and Google to school districts and independent schools. She is a TEDx speaker with more than fifteen years of experience presenting at local, regional, and international conferences.

Lainie's work has been highlighted in many publications, including Edutopia, *OC Family* magazine, ASCD K–12 Leadership SmartBrief, Getting Smart, and PBS NewsHour. Since 2014, Lainie has been a consultant for the Orange County Department of Education's Institute for Leadership Development.

Lainie is the lead author of the book *Evolving Learner: Shifting From Professional Development to Professional Learning From Kids, Peers, and the World* and a contributing author of *Because of a Teacher: Stories of the Past to Inspire the Future of Education.*

Connect with Lainie
LainieRowell.com
Social Media: @LainieRowell

Bring Lainie to Your Organization or Event!

Popular Topics from Lainie Rowell:

- Evolving with Gratitude: Three Ways to Use Gratitude to Promote Well-Being & Improve Learning
- Evolving Learner: Cultivating a Culture of Transparency and Agency in Learning
- Inquiry-Based Learning: Discover, Discuss, Demonstrate
- Three Social-Emotional Learning (SEL) Practices We Can Do Every Day
- Innovative Leadership: Cultivating a Culture of Ongoing, Personalized Professional Learning
- Building and Maintaining Community to Engage and Motivate Students in Online and Blended Learning

To book Lainie Rowell to speak at your event, visit LainieRowell.com

About the Contributors

Dwight Carter is an award-winning and nationally recognized school leader. He is the director of student support systems for the Eastland-Fairfield Career and Technical School District.

He is the coauthor of *What's in Your Space?: Five Steps for Better School and Classroom Design* and *Leading Schools in Disruptive Times: How to Survive Hyper-change.* He is also a contributing author to George Couros's *Because of a Teacher.* His first solo book, *Be Great: Five Principles to Power Your Legacy as an Educator*, will be released in 2022.

You can connect with Dwight on Twitter @Dwight_Carter, or email mrdwightcarter@gmail.com.

Livia Chan is a head teacher, presenter, and member of the Teach Better team. She is a contributing author of *Because of a Teacher* who is deeply passionate about writing, the gift of relationships, and leading with heart. Livia believes that in every atomic interaction, we have the opportunity to uplift others through our kindness and gratitude. She would love to connect with you on Twitter at @LiviaChanL or at livchan.com.

Chey Cheney and Pav Wander are two middle school teachers from Toronto, Canada. They have a passion for elevating and amplifying student voice while honoring their lived experiences and identities. Their podcast, *The Chey and Pav Show*, and their live radio show, *The Drive*, on VoicEd Radio, take educators and listeners through the ins and outs of the fields of teaching, learning, and leadership. Drawn to their anecdotal and inviting banter laced with caring insightfulness, listeners engage in conversations that are surely eye-opening and impactful and that tackle some of the real, sometimes difficult, and ever-changing issues in education! Over the past two years, the dynamic duo have learned alongside the vast professional learning community of educators around the world, and have been gifted the opportunity to share their learning through presentations and seminars all around Canada and the United States. Chey and Pav are also authors of the teaching resource book *Teachers Talking Teaching*, as well as a children's book, *The Magnificent Microphone*.

George Couros is a worldwide leader in the area of innovative teaching, learning, and leading, and has a focus on innovation as a human endeavor. He has worked at all levels of education, from K–12 as a teacher, technology facilitator, and school and district administrator, to his current role of adjunct instructor with the Graduate School of Education at the University of Pennsylvania. George is the author of the books *The Innovator's Mindset*, *Innovate Inside the Box*, and his latest release, *Because of a Teacher*. He is also a very proud dad.

Paige Couros is an experienced elementary educator and an innovative entrepreneur. Passionate about teaching and learning, Paige amplifies the voices of educators around the world as a leader of IMPress, a publishing company. The mother of two amazing little girls, Paige shares inspiring ways to promote learning through play on Instagram @teach.me.mom. You can also connect with Paige on Twitter and Instagram @PaigeCouros.

Rachelle Dené Poth is an edtech consultant, presenter, attorney, author, and Spanish and STEAM emerging technology teacher. Rachelle has a Juris Doctor degree from Duquesne University School of Law, a master's in instructional technology and is pursuing a second doctorate in educational technology. Rachelle is an ISTE certified educator  and recipient of ISTE's Making It Happen Award. She has also received several presidential gold and silver awards for volunteer service. She is a blogger and the author of seven books.

Jennifer Evans is a full-time emergency room nurse with a master's of science in nursing. She is also an experienced homeschool educator, as well as the wife of a fire chief and mother of two girls. During her service as president of her public school's Parent Teacher Student Association  (PTSA), she focused on community building and inclusive practices to promote psychological and physical safety for all adults and students to thrive. Jennifer continues to serve on her public school's PTSA board and regularly volunteers her time to help others in her community.

Sean Gaillard is an educator, administrator, author, keynote speaker, and podcaster. Gaillard is currently principal of Moore Magnet Elementary School in Winston-Salem, North Carolina. Sean is the author of *The Pepper Effect* and contributing author of *Education Write Now, Volume II*. He is the host of *The Principal Liner Notes* podcast.

Follow Sean on Twitter and Instagram @smgaillard.

An experienced leader in education, strategy, culture development, and implementation, Brianna Henneke Hodges helps develop and enact human-centered transformational strategies that personalize experience, elevate engagement, and enhance outcomes. She was named a K–12 Administrator to Watch (2018) and Texas EdTech  of the Year (2017). Brianna is also a national adviser and spokesperson for Future Ready Instructional Leaders, a Future Ready faculty member, cohost of the *Lemonade Learning* podcast, and host of *Learning Through Uncertainty*, a Future Ready Schools podcast.

Lauren Kaufman is an educator whose professional passion is to empower teachers to lead and develop lifelong literacy practices in all learners. She has served as an elementary classroom teacher, literacy specialist, instructional coach, and mentor coordinator. She is currently an assistant principal in Long Island, NY. Lauren has led  teams developing units of study in reading and writing, has provided educators with job-embedded professional learning, and guides new teachers with acclimating to school systems. She is also a contributor to *Because of a Teacher*. You can connect with Lauren on Twitter @Lau7210 or her website, laurenmkaufman.com.

Dr. Katie Martin is the chief impact officer at Learner-Centered Collaborative and author of *Evolving Education* and *Learner-Centered Innovation*. She has served as a middle school English language arts teacher, instructional coach, and leader of the district's new teacher mentoring  program. Dr. Martin works in diverse contexts to learn, research, and support authentic and purposeful learning for all students. As a mom, she wants her kids to have learning experiences in school that build on their strengths and interests, and as an educator, she is passionate about making sure we do the same for all kids.

Tara Martin is an enthusiastic educator, keynote speaker, and author who thrives on change and refuses to settle for the status quo. She has served as a classroom teacher, an instructional coach, and a district administrator. Tara's passion for education and love of writing led her to her current role, where she coaches and serves educational authors as the director of public relations and communication for Dave Burgess Consulting, Inc.

Martin's ambition is to lead a culture of innovative change, keep social-emotional learning at the heart of her work, and motivate others to become the best they can be, all while staying *real* and yet never reaching a plateau.

Katie Novak, EdD, is an internationally renowned education consultant, author, graduate instructor at the University of Pennsylvania, and former assistant superintendent of schools. With twenty years of experience in teaching and administration, an earned doctorate in curriculum and teaching, and ten published books, Katie designs and presents workshops nationally and internationally that focus on the implementation of inclusive practices, UDL, multitiered systems of support, and universally designed leadership.

Bobby Pollicino is an educator, school leader, writer, and presenter. He is the author of *Principled Leader*, due out in the fall of 2022. Bobby has more than twenty years of experience as an educator, coach, and school leader. His expertise includes meeting culture, team building, and wellness. Bobby has presented locally and nationally on these topics. He is currently head of the upper school at Bullis in Potomac, Maryland. Bobby strives to be a better husband, father, leader, teammate, and person every day. You can connect with Bobby on Twitter @BobbyPollicino or on LinkedIn.

Tisha Richmond is a district student engagement and professional development specialist, Canva learning consultant, national speaker, and author from Southern Oregon. She taught career and technical education for twenty-five years and has served in various leadership roles regionally and nationally. Tisha is the author of the book *Make Learning MAGICAL*, which unlocks seven keys to transform teaching and create unforgettable experiences in the classroom. She speaks nationally on a variety of topics related to teaching and learning.

Stacey Roshan is an educator, speaker, consultant, and author of *Tech with Heart: Leveraging Technology to Empower Student Voice, Ease Anxiety, & Create Compassionate Classrooms.* She is passionate about discovering and sharing innovative ways to leverage technology to deepen relationships, build confidence, and create a safe learning environment where every student feels empowered to share their voice. Her work has been featured in *USA Today* and the *Washington Post* and on CNN. You can connect with Stacey on Twitter @buddyxo or on her website, techiemusings.com.

Stephanie Rothstein is an edtech TOSA in Northern California, an educational consultant, writer, and TEDxer. Stephanie's favorite projects are ones that create innovative opportunities; she was the chair of a design thinking pathway for over ten years. Stephanie is the creator of CanWeTalkEDU, founder of Global GEG, and a

Google innovator. Her writing can be found in Edutopia, *Because of a Teacher*, and on her blog. Connect with her on Twitter and Instagram @StephRothEDU or on her website, StephRothEDU.com.

Joshua Stamper is a middle school assistant principal for a North Texas school district, where he works with students in grades six to eight. Prior to Joshua's current position, he was a classroom art educator and athletic coach.

　　In addition to being an administrator, Joshua is a podcaster, leadership coach, education presenter, and podcast network manager for the Teach Better team. He is also the author of *Aspire to Lead*.

Naomi Toland is an educator, podcaster, Google innovator, and self-proclaimed travel addict. She is passionate about exploring ways we can learn about our brains and bodies to empathize and understand ourselves and those around us. Naomi has experience working across the pri-

mary sector, having worked alongside learners aged two to thirteen, and she has a love for exploring different cultures, having lived and taught in London, Tokyo, and Auckland.

　　Naomi leads #Empathetic_Educators, a global community inquiring into all things NERDY (Neuroscience, Empathy, Relationships, Design Thinking) and much more. You can keep up to date on her website, naomitoland.com, or @naomi_toland on Twitter.

More from

IMPRESS

ImpressBooks.org

Empower
What Happens when Students Own Their Learning
by A.J. Juliani and John Spencer

Learner-Centered Innovation
Spark Curiosity, Ignite Passion, and Unleash Genius
by Katie Martin

Unleash Talent
Bringing Out the Best in Yourself and the Learners You Serve
by Kara Knollmeyer

Reclaiming Our Calling
Hold On to the Heart, Mind, and Hope of Education
by Brad Gustafson

Take the L.E.A.P.
Ignite a Culture of Innovation
by Elisabeth Bostwick

Drawn to Teach
An Illustrated Guide to Transforming Your Teaching
written by Josh Stumpenhorst and illustrated by Trevor Guthke

Math Recess
Playful Learning in an Age of Disruption
by Sunil Singh and Dr. Christopher Brownell

Innovate inside the Box
Empowering Learners Through UDL and Innovator's Mindset
by George Couros and Katie Novak

Personal & Authentic
Designing Learning Experiences That Last a Lifetime
by Thomas C. Murray

Learner-Centered Leadership
A Blueprint for Transformational Change in Learning Communities
by Devin Vodicka

Kids These Days
*A Game Plan for (Re)Connecting with Those We
Teach, Lead & Love*
by Dr. Jody Carrington

UDL and Blended Learning
Thriving in Flexible Learning Landscapes
by Katie Novak and Catlin Tucker

Teachers These Days
Stories & Strategies for Reconnection
by Dr. Jody Carrington and Laurie McIntosh

Because of a Teacher
Stories of the Past to Inspire the Future of Education
written and curated by George Couros

Evolving Education
Shifting to a Learner-Centered Paradigm
by Katie Martin

Adaptable
*How to Create an Adaptable Curriculum and Flexible Learning
Experiences That Work in Any Environment*
by A.J. Juliani

Lead from Where You Are
Building Intention, Connection, and Direction in Our Schools
by Joe Sanfelippo

CPSIA information can be obtained
at www.ICGtesting.com
Printed in the USA
BVHW030451080622
639021BV00005B/21